I0200927

RELATIONAL ACUITY 1.0

Masterminding Kingdom Relationships

Tiffany Buckner

Relational Acuity 1.0
Masterminding Kingdom Relationships

©2022, Tiffany Buckner
www.tiffanybuckner.com
info@tiffanybuckner.com

Published by Anointed Fire House

Edited by:
Anointed Fire House
J. Junga
New Pointe Editing

ISBN: 978-1-955557-24-5

This book contains material protected under International and Federal Copyright Laws and Treaties. Any unauthorized reprint or use of this material is prohibited. No part of this book may be reproduced or transmitted in any form or by any means, electronic or mechanical, including photocopying, recording, or by any information storage and retrieval system without express written permission from the author/publisher.

Although the author and publisher have made every effort to ensure that the information in this book was correct at press time, the author and publisher do not assume and hereby disclaim any liability to any party for any loss, damage, or disruption caused by errors or omissions, whether such errors or omissions result from negligence, accident, or any other cause.

Unless otherwise noted, Scripture quotations are taken from The Holy Bible, New King James Version® (NKJV). Copyright© 1982 by Thomas Nelson. Used by permission. All rights reserved. Scriptures taken from the NEW AMERICAN STANDARD BIBLE®,

Copyright©1960,1962,1963,1968,1971,1972,1973,1975,1977,1995 by The Lockman Foundation. Used by permission.

Scripture quotations marked NIV are taken from The Holy Bible, New International Version ®, NIV ®, Copyright 1973, 1978, 1984, 2001 by Biblica, Inc.™ Used by permission. All rights reserved. Scriptures marked AMP are taken from the AMPLIFIED BIBLE (AMP): Scripture taken from the AMPLIFIED® BIBLE, Copyright © 1954, 1958, 1962, 1964, 1965, 1987 by the Lockman Foundation Used by Permission. (www.Lockman.org)

Scripture quotations marked NLT are taken from The Holy Bible, New Living Translation, Copyright© 1996. Used by permission of Tyndale House Publishers, Inc., Wheaton, Illinois 60189. All rights reserved.

Scripture quotations marked MSG, or The Message are taken from The Holy Bible, The Message. Copyright© 1993, 1994, 1995, 1996, 2000, 2001, 2002 by NavPress Publishing Group. Used by permission. All rights reserved.

Scripture quotations marked ESV are taken from The Holy Bible, English Standard Version®. English Standard Version are registered trademarks of Crossway®.

TABLE OF CONTENTS

What is Relational Acuity?............................1

Roles and Responsibilities..........................9

Consumers vs. Producers............................31

Understanding Voids..................................43

Intimate Spaces.......................................53

Intellectual Spaces..................................65

Relational Labels....................................75

Relational Protocol..................................93

Relational Poverty..................................105

Familiarity and Dishonor...........................117

Trauma Bonds and Soul Ties........................139

Narcissist Magnets..................................153

Testing the Spirit..................................167

Crabs in a Bucket..................................173

Objectification.....................................187

Generalization......................................201

Masterminding Kingdom Relationships...............209

INTRODUCTION

Relational Acuity: Masterminding Kingdom Relationships (Part I) is a masterfully written book designed to give you the language of relationships.

In the western world, most of us have never been taught one of the most vital lessons in life, survival, success and mental strength, and that is—how to categorize and respond to the many relationships (familial, platonic, professional and romantic) that we find ourselves a part of. Because of this, we don't know the language of relationships, we are almost always healing from some form of trauma and the mental health industry is thriving. As a matter of fact, mental and substance abuse centers have almost doubled in revenue in the last ten years, and those numbers are rapidly inclining. Nevertheless, God has given us the blueprint for relationships through the many stories and commandments found in our Bibles. The problem is—many of us are slaves of culture. All the same, our traditions encourage or allow us to fit into the sectors of society that we inhabit or frequent. However, if we are bold enough to challenge or forsake those traditions, Satan has taught many of the people we love to weaponize one of the most prevalent, efficient and evil spirits to ever walk the Earth, and that is—the spirit of rejection.

Relational Acuity: Masterminding Kingdom Relationships is written to help you to break free from the chains of oppression brought on by toxic, ungodly, narcissistic and demonic relationships. As the first book in the Relational Acuity series, Masterminding Kingdom Relationships can best be described as a book of language. In this compelling and dexterous guide, you will learn the science of the spiritual world and come to understand how to properly position people in your life so that you can flourish and experience Heaven on Earth.

What is Relational Acuity?

I want you to imagine yourself standing inside of a jar. That jar represents your circle or, better yet, your intimate space. Inside that jar, you'd find the people you hold near and dear to your heart. Outside of that jar, you'd find people that you are familiar with. Some of these people don't have intimate access to you because:

1. You don't know them that well.
2. You don't want to know them personally or intimately (or vice versa).
3. You once knew them intimately and decided that they were too immature or too broken to have that measure of access to you (or vice versa).
4. They are connected with people you don't want to personally affiliate yourself with.
5. They remind you of someone you've had a negative experience with.
6. You're intimidated by them (or vice versa).
7. You simply don't have time to connect with them intimately.

Of course, there are many more reasons why you've kept some people out of your intimate circle. Understand this —your heart has a chemical makeup, and by chemical, I am referring to your beliefs, traumas and everything that comes together to form your belief system. The same is true for every human on the face of this planet. And when two or more people come together and express themselves, their beliefs begin to interact. If they do not agree, a chemical reaction occurs, either in the form of anger (explosion) or apathy/disinterest (neutralization). If they do agree, a relationship is formed. Howbeit, we are always learning; this means that a person who positively impacts us today can negatively affect us tomorrow. This is why so many people on the face of this planet are not mentally, emotionally, physically or spiritually healthy. We've all been taught to hold onto people who've played a positive role in our lives, even when their seasons have expired. Consequently, we come across people every day who are on the edge of their sanity, people who feel like they are about to explode. Of course, this has everything to do with the people around them. This is why we need relational acuity.

What is relational acuity or relational intelligence? To answer this question, we have to first understand the root word of "relational," which, of course, is "relation." According to Oxford Languages, the word "relation" means "the way in which two or more concepts, objects, or people are connected; a thing's effect on or relevance to another." Oxford Languages defines "acuity" as "sharpness or keenness of thought, vision, or hearing." The word "intelligence" is defined as "the ability to acquire and apply knowledge and skills" (Source: Oxford Languages). Therefore, this would mean that the phrase "relational acuity" could be defined in the most simplistic way as "the sharp, intentional or strategic application of knowledge gained in relationships." The truth is, one of the reasons there are so many hurting people on the face of this planet is because most of us lack relational intelligence. In short, we weren't taught how to relate to people, how to differentiate a friend from a foe and what seasonal relationships look like. Instead, we were taught what I refer to as "toxic loyalty" (more on this later). We were taught to fight through all the obstacles and hold on to people, regardless of what they've done to us, not realizing that just like milk sours once it has expired, relationships do the same. And this isn't to say that every souring or frustrating relationship is bereft of life, after all, every relationship will have its ups and downs. But we have to learn to discern what relationships are lifelong, which ones are seasonal and which ones are demonic, for lack of a better word.

Most of us are aware of the story of David and Jonathan. Jonathan was King Saul's son, and of course, Saul eventually became jealous of David. Consequently, he plotted to kill David, and this caused David to go on the run. Amazingly enough, Jonathan helped David to escape his father's wrath. Let's look at a few scriptures.
- **1 Samuel 18:1:** And it came to pass, when he had made an end of speaking unto Saul, that the soul of Jonathan was knit with the soul of David, and Jonathan loved him as his own soul.
- **1 Samuel 19:1-7:** And Saul spake to Jonathan his

son, and to all his servants, that they should kill David. But Jonathan Saul's son delighted much in David: and Jonathan told David, saying, Saul my father seeketh to kill thee: now therefore, I pray thee, take heed to thyself until the morning, and abide in a secret place, and hide thyself: And I will go out and stand beside my father in the field where thou art, and I will commune with my father of thee; and what I see, that I will tell thee. And Jonathan spake good of David unto Saul his father, and said unto him, Let not the king sin against his servant, against David; because he hath not sinned against thee, and because his works have been to theeward very good: For he did put his life in his hand, and slew the Philistine, and the LORD wrought a great salvation for all Israel: thou sawest it, and didst rejoice: wherefore then wilt thou sin against innocent blood, to slay David without a cause? And Saul hearkened unto the voice of Jonathan: and Saul sware, As the LORD liveth, he shall not be slain. And Jonathan called David, and Jonathan shewed him all those things. And Jonathan brought David to Saul, and he was in his presence, as in times past.

- **1 Samuel 19:8-10:** And there was war again: and David went out, and fought with the Philistines, and slew them with a great slaughter; and they fled from him. And the evil spirit from the LORD was upon Saul, as he sat in his house with his javelin in his hand: and David played with his hand. And Saul sought to smite David even to the wall with the javelin; but he slipped away out of Saul's presence, and he smote the javelin into the wall: and David fled, and escaped that night.

- 1 Samuel 20:1-10: And David fled from Naioth in Ramah, and came and said before Jonathan, What have I done? what is mine iniquity? and what is my sin before thy father, that he seeketh my life? And he said unto him, God forbid; thou shalt not die: behold, my father will do nothing either great or small, but that he will shew it me: and why should my father hide this thing from me? it is not so. And David sware moreover, and said, Thy father certainly knoweth that I have found grace in thine eyes; and he saith, Let not Jonathan know this, lest he be grieved: but truly as the LORD liveth, and as thy soul liveth, there is but a step between me and death. Then said Jonathan unto David, Whatsoever thy soul desireth, I will even do it for thee. And David said unto Jonathan, Behold, to morrow is the new moon, and I should not fail to sit with the king at meat: but let me go, that I may hide myself in the field unto the third day at even. If thy father at all miss me, then say, David earnestly asked leave of me that he might run to Bethlehem his city: for there is a yearly sacrifice there for all the family. If he say thus, It is well; thy servant shall have peace: but if he be very wroth, then be sure that evil is determined by him. Therefore thou shalt deal kindly with thy servant; for thou hast brought thy servant into a covenant of the LORD with thee: notwithstanding, if there be in me iniquity, slay me thyself; for why shouldest thou bring me to thy father? And Jonathan said, Far be it from thee: for if I knew certainly that evil were determined by my father to come upon thee, then would not I tell it thee? Then said David to Jonathan, Who shall tell me? or what if thy father answer thee roughly?

Of course, this is not the entirety of the story. David would eventually have to go on the run from Saul and Jonathan would help him to escape his father's death-grip. This act alone would almost get Jonathan killed. But the question is—was it even possible for Jonathan to divide his loyalties? Could Jonathan truly remain a friend of David's, all the while serving as an honorable son to his father, King Saul? The answer is no. Look at the following scriptures.

- **1 John 4:20:** If a man say, I love God, and hateth his brother, he is a liar: for he that loveth not his brother whom he hath seen, how can he love God whom he hath not seen?
- **James 4:4:** Ye adulterers and adulteresses, know ye not that the friendship of the world is enmity with God? Whosoever therefore will be a friend of the world is the enemy of God.

While these scriptures deal with our loyalty towards God,

they also help us to understand the very foundation of loyalty. David represents the Kingdom of God; Saul, on the other hand, represents rebellion or, better yet, the kingdom of darkness. Jonathan did not forsake all that he had to follow David and fight with him. He simply favored him for a season and he extended mercy to David. But because his loyalties could not be divided, ultimately, Jonathan (more than likely) became David's enemy. As a matter of fact, some theologians believe that David was referring to Jonathan when he wrote Psalm 41:9. It reads, "Yea, mine own familiar friend, in whom I trusted, which did eat of my bread, hath lifted up his heel against me." The Bible didn't mention any other close friends of David except Jonathan. Why is this important or even relevant? Because if we are going to grow in our relational acuity, we must understand that human beings are incapable of hosting two opposing relationships. This isn't to say that we can't be mutually connected to two people who are at enmity with one another; this is to say that we will agree with one of those people and disagree or largely disagree with the other. And when we don't mature relationally, we set the stage for hurt, betrayal and repeated bouts of disappointment. This is how people become bitter, distrusting, suspicious of others and unforgiving. Everyone on the face of this planet is not evil, but whenever we don't grow in our relational acuity, we will often keep surrounding ourselves with the same types of people and consequently suffer through the same results. This is called a cycle, a habit and a stronghold. The world calls this insanity. One of the most interesting definitions of insanity is—doing the same thing again and again, and expecting a different result. It is then safe to say that most of the people on the face of this planet, by this definition, are insane. To maintain peace, we must understand the different types of relationships and which category each person in our lives fits into. This is relational acuity.

ROLES AND RESPONSIBILITIES

Throughout your life, you will meet people who are spiritually nearsighted as it relates to you and people who are spiritually farsighted. Remember, nearsighted people see objects that are close to them clearly, but things and people that are afar off are relatively blurry to them. On the other hand, farsighted people see people and things from afar clearly, but anything and any person that is close to them is relatively blurry. People are the same way. Some people see you better from afar, and by this, I mean they can see your potential, see your good character, recognize your anointing and respect how intentional you are as a human being. But if you bring them close, they may quickly become your enemies. Then again, some people can only see just how marvelous (or unstable) you are from up close, but from afar, they will often prejudge you, fear engaging with you and even misunderstand you. And, of course, there are those who have perfect vision. They see your potential and value from up close and from afar. These people, of course, are rare and we don't often meet them in our day-to-day dealings. They are typically God-sends; these are the people who we'll likely form lifelong alliances with, either through friendships, brotherhoods/sisterhoods or maybe even marriage. Nevertheless, because these people are so few and far between, it is easy for us to consider lowering our standards, reasoning within ourselves that we may be too picky, too demanding, or just want too much for ourselves whenever we find ourselves ending or entering other relationships. And while this may be true for some people, the greatest test of this is—are you simply requiring what you're offering or are you being hypocritical? For example, I need to take better care of myself physically. While I have had a gym membership for about three years, I haven't been to the gym in about two of those years. It's silly, but it's true. It would be irrational for me to demand that any guy who wants to pursue me romantically be fit. Would I be wrong to require this? No, just irrational. Consequently, I could potentially cause a significant delay in my life by requiring of someone what I have not required of myself.

You are a spirit and your life is a system. What is a system? Check out the following definitions:
- **Collins Dictionary**: A system is a way of working, organizing, or doing something which follows a fixed plan or set of rules.
- **Cambridge Dictionary**: a set of connected things or devices that operate together.
- **Vocabulary.com**: A system is a group of things that connect and form some kind of coherent whole.
- **Merriam Webster**: a regularly interacting or interdependent group of items forming a unified whole.
- **Oxford Languages**: a set of things working

together as parts of a mechanism or an interconnecting network.

Romans 8:28 states, "And we know that all things work together for good to them that love God, to them who are the called according to his purpose." This scripture is referencing a system. Notice that it says "all things" work together for good to them who love God who are called according to His purpose. This includes all of the evil we've suffered in our lives. All the same, this means that all things do not work together for the good to them who do not love God. Yes, this includes Christians who profess Christ but do not have His heart. In other words, they can, do and will deal with a great deal of opposition, but this opposition isn't God's way of punishing them. Instead, this is His way of protecting them, correcting them and challenging their perspectives. And while all things work for our good, we have to admit that some of the lessons we've learned didn't feel good when we were in the classrooms of life. We've learned (the hard way) about ignoring red flags, tolerating toxic people, moving too fast in relationships and the list goes on. Then again, maybe we haven't fully learned our lessons yet. Either way, the Bible says that it will all eventually work for our good. Howbeit, it is absolutely imperative to our mental health that we are intentional! What does it mean to be intentional?

1. To become the blessings we want to attract.
2. To treat everyone in our lives with love, honor and respect.

3. To forgive from the heart and not from our intellect.

4. To make a purposeful effort to heal so that we won't hurt the people in our lives or the people who will someday share space and time with us.

5. To get deliverance whenever we need it (note: if you don't believe in deliverance, just move on to the next step).

6. To apologize when we need to. In other words, to never exalt our feelings and emotions over the feelings and emotions of others; we must be both considerate and empathetic.

7. To take accountability for our wrongs and make the necessary adjustments to ensure that we don't repeat those infractions.

8. To reflect God's love in everything that we do and say.

9. To be prudent, planning ahead of time to ensure that everything we do runs smoothly.

10. To count the costs of everything we build before we start building it; this way, we won't have a bunch of unfinished projects and a string of broken relationships on our trails.

In every system, there are parts and functions, all of which have roles to complete in order to carry out the system's main objective. For example, I recently came across a video of a bread-making machine. At the start of the video, a computer screen was opened, showing three machines, all of which are interconnected. All the machines are numbered, with the first machine being listed as number one. After this take, the video cuts to show a large batch of dough being mixed in one of the machines. After this, the video shows the dough already formed into the shape of biscuits being lifted from one machine to the other through a conveyor belt, while more dough is being dumped into the machine. The bread then falls through a series of holes, and from there, they are individually picked up by what appears to be small bowls. They then go onto another conveyor belt where they are further shaped by a metal belt, and as they pass to the next level, they are seasoned a little more with flour. The video is more than ten minutes in length, and rather than bore you with the details, I'll sum it up this way—the video ends with the bread being stretched and rolled into croissants by the machine, and then baked. This is what I picture anytime I think of the concept of a system.

Every function of that machine is necessary, and if one of those processes were skipped, the bread would likely be deformed, inedible or even potentially dangerous to consume. Additionally, there is order in the process. The bread can't go in the oven first; it has to go through a series of steps before it reaches the oven. Compare this concept to your life. Everyone in your life is a part of your system. Systems need a specific order to function properly. Everyone in your life has a role and a responsibility. Some people have to remain at a distance because they are farsighted. If you bring them too close, they will jam or delay the system of your life. Some people have to be brought close if you want to see growth in your life. The problem with most of us is—we lack relational acuity, and because of this, we oftentimes bring people close who don't have the spiritual maturity or emotional capacity to walk alongside us. All the same, I've noticed a pattern with a lot of believers today. They push people away or avoid people who they know would challenge them to live more intentional and Godly lives. They do this by mislabeling those people so that they can justify remaining in a bunch of expired relationships. People don't like change; many of them are terrified of it. But change is necessary if we want to reach our greatest potential and become who God designed us to be. Remember, faith without works is dead!

Everyone who enters your life or is a part of your life should have a measure of distance to and away from your heart. Not all relationships are designed to be intimate. Some relationships are seasonal, some relationships are designed to help you perform a single function and some relationships are permanent. Once that function has been completed, you may never see or walk with that person again. A good example of a seasonal relationship was the relationship between Elijah and the widow woman. She had an assignment in his life, and he had an assignment in her life. Let's look at that story (note: if you are familiar with the story and don't want to read it again, you can skip the following scripture reading):

- **1 Kings 17:8-24:** And the word of the LORD came unto him, saying, Arise, get thee to Zarephath, which belongeth to Zidon, and dwell there: behold, I have commanded a widow woman there to sustain thee. So he arose and went to Zarephath. And when he came to the gate of the city, behold, the widow woman was there gathering of sticks: and he called to her, and said, Fetch me, I pray thee, a little water in a vessel, that I may drink. And as she was going to fetch it, he called to her, and said, Bring me, I pray thee, a morsel of bread in thine hand. And she said, As the LORD thy God liveth, I have not a cake, but an handful of meal in a barrel, and a little oil in a cruse: and, behold, I am gathering two sticks, that I may go in and dress it for me and my son, that we may eat it, and die. And Elijah said unto her, Fear not; go and do as thou hast said: but make me thereof a little cake first, and bring it unto me, and after make for thee and for thy son. For thus saith the LORD God of Israel, The barrel of meal shall not waste, neither shall the cruse of oil fail, until the day that the LORD sendeth rain upon the earth. And she went and did according to the saying of Elijah: and she, and he, and her house, did eat many days. And the barrel of meal wasted not, neither did the cruse of oil fail, according to the word of the LORD, which he spake by Elijah. And it came to pass after these things, that the son of the woman, the mistress of the house, fell sick; and his sickness was so sore, that there was no breath left in him. And she said unto Elijah, What have I to do with thee, O thou man of God? art thou come unto me to call my sin to remembrance, and to slay my son? And he said unto her, Give me thy son. And he took him out of her bosom, and carried him up into a loft, where he abode, and laid him upon his own bed. And he cried unto the LORD, and said, O LORD my God, hast thou also brought evil upon the widow with whom I sojourn, by slaying her son? And he stretched himself upon the child three times, and cried unto the LORD, and said, O LORD my God, I pray thee, let this child's soul come into him again. And the LORD heard the voice of Elijah; and the soul of the child came into him again, and he revived. And Elijah took the child, and brought him down out of the chamber into the house, and delivered him unto his mother: and Elijah said, See, thy son liveth. And the woman said to Elijah, Now by this I know that thou art a man of God, and that the word of the LORD in thy mouth is truth.

Another good example of a single-function relationship is the relationship between Rahab and the spies. Below, you'll find the story. Note: if you are familiar with the story and don't want to read it again, you can skip the following scriptures.

- **Joshua 2:1-21:**And Joshua the son of Nun sent out

of Shittim two men to spy secretly, saying, Go view
the land, even Jericho. And they went, and came
into an harlot's house, named Rahab, and lodged
there. And it was told the king of Jericho, saying,
Behold, there came men in hither to night of the
children of Israel to search out the country. And the
king of Jericho sent unto Rahab, saying, Bring forth
the men that are come to thee, which are entered
into thine house: for they be come to search out all
the country. And the woman took the two men, and
hid them, and said thus, There came men unto me,
but I wist not whence they were: And it came to
pass about the time of shutting of the gate, when it
was dark, that the men went out: whither the men
went I wot not: pursue after them quickly; for ye
shall overtake them. But she had brought them up
to the roof of the house, and hid them with the
stalks of flax, which she had laid in order upon the
roof. And the men pursued after them the way to
Jordan unto the fords: and as soon as they which
pursued after them were gone out, they shut the
gate. And before they were laid down, she came up
unto them upon the roof; And she said unto the
men, I know that the LORD hath given you the land,
and that your terror is fallen upon us, and that all
the inhabitants of the land faint because of you. For
we have heard how the LORD dried up the water of
the Red sea for you, when ye came out of Egypt;
and what ye did unto the two kings of the Amorites,

that were on the other side Jordan, Sihon and Og, whom ye utterly destroyed. And as soon as we had heard these things, our hearts did melt, neither did there remain any more courage in any man, because of you: for the LORD your God, he is God in heaven above, and in earth beneath. Now therefore, I pray you, swear unto me by the LORD, since I have shewed you kindness, that ye will also shew kindness unto my father's house, and give me a true token: And that ye will save alive my father, and my mother, and my brethren, and my sisters, and all that they have, and deliver our lives from death. And the men answered her, Our life for yours, if ye utter not this our business. And it shall be, when the LORD hath given us the land, that we will deal kindly and truly with thee. Then she let them down by a cord through the window: for her house was upon the town wall, and she dwelt upon the wall. And she said unto them, Get you to the mountain, lest the pursuers meet you; and hide yourselves there three days, until the pursuers be returned: and afterward may ye go your way. And the men said unto her, We will be blameless of this thine oath which thou hast made us swear. Behold, when we come into the land, thou shalt bind this line of scarlet thread in the window which thou didst let us down by: and thou shalt bring thy father, and thy mother, and thy brethren, and all thy father's household, home unto thee. And it shall be, that whosoever shall go out of the doors of thy house into the street, his blood shall be upon his head, and we will be guiltless: and whosoever shall be with thee in the house, his blood shall be on our head, if any hand be upon him. And if thou utter this our business, then we will be quit of thine oath which thou hast made us to swear. And she said, According unto your words, so be it. And she sent them away, and they departed: and she bound the scarlet line in the window.

- **Joshua 6:15-25:** And it came to pass on the seventh day, that they rose early about the dawning of the day, and compassed the city after the same manner seven times: only on that day they compassed the city seven times. And it came to pass at the seventh time, when the priests blew with the trumpets, Joshua said unto the people, Shout; for the LORD hath given you the city. And the city shall be accursed, even it, and all that are therein, to the LORD: only Rahab the harlot shall live, she and all that are with her in the house, because she hid the messengers that we sent. And ye, in any wise keep yourselves from the accursed thing, lest ye make yourselves accursed, when ye take of the accursed thing, and make the camp of Israel a curse, and trouble it. But all the silver, and gold, and vessels of brass and iron, are consecrated unto the LORD: they shall come into the treasury of the LORD. So the people shouted when the priests blew with the trumpets: and it came to pass, when the people heard the sound of the trumpet, and the people shouted with a great shout, that the wall fell down flat, so that the people went up into the city, every man straight before him, and they took the city. And they utterly destroyed all that was in the city, both man and woman, young and old, and ox, and sheep, and ass, with the edge of the sword. But Joshua had said unto the two men that had spied out the country, Go into the harlot's house, and bring out thence the woman, and all that she hath, as ye sware unto her. And the young men that were spies went in, and brought out Rahab, and her father, and her mother, and her brethren, and all that she had; and they brought out all her kindred, and left them without the camp of Israel. And they burnt the city with fire, and all that was therein: only the silver, and the gold, and the vessels of brass and of iron, they put into the treasury of the house of the LORD. And Joshua saved Rahab the harlot alive, and her father's household, and all that she had; and she dwelleth in Israel even unto this day; because she hid the messengers, which Joshua sent to spy out Jericho.

Of course, a good example of a permanent or multi-function relationship would be the relationship between a man and his wife. Then again, there are some platonic relationships that are lifelong. If you want to function at your fullest potential, you have to differentiate one from another. Because of loneliness, rejection and whatever other issues we're hosting, we sometimes give permanent roles to temporary people. This is why we spend a great portion of our lives healing and recovering from the trauma of failed relationships. Nevertheless, all things work together for our good, so we should have, at minimum, learned our lessons. However, in truth, a lot of people don't take accountability for their roles in their own pain. Consequently, they find themselves jamming up the systems of their lives, thus causing themselves to go in cycles and circles. A jammed-up system is called a stronghold.

How do we know who should be close and who should remain at a distance? After all, the Bible told us to guard our hearts. In short, most of the relationships we form in life will be intellectual; very few will be intimate. And, of course, by intimate, I mean both close and personal. With intellectual relationships, people will get to know you, but in intimate relationships, people will come to understand you. What's the difference? Knowledge puffs up, according to 1 Corinthians 8:1, and to puff up means to be made prideful. How many prideful people feel comfortable enough with you to be disrespectful, dishonorable or simply not reciprocate whatever it is that you bring to the relationship? If you did an inventory of your life, chances are, you'd likely find quite a few crooks in your intimate space. But get this—from afar, they wouldn't be crooks because they wouldn't have personal access to you. From afar, they would likely turn out to be great fixtures in your life, and they could perform the functions that God has designed or assigned them to accomplish, and vice versa. But you brought them close to you, and because of this, their view of you is relatively blurry. So, your relationship with them may be filled with the following:

1. Offense.
2. Pointless conversations.
3. Unrealistic expectations.
4. Exploitation.
5. Hurt.

This doesn't always mean that they're bad people. Sometimes, it means that you've entrusted a broken or immature person with a responsibility that was and is far too complicated for them. Think of it this way—imagine that you're the owner of a Fortune 500 company that brings in over 300 million dollars a year. Would you hire a high school dropout to be your Chief of Operations? Probably not, but why? It's simple. You know that while the child in question may very well be intelligent and maybe even mature for his age, he's still a child and doesn't have the education needed to operate in such an important role. All the same, he'd likely be highly impressionable and immature. You'd most likely look for someone who has the experience and history at excelling in the role that you want him or her to function in. Why don't we think this way in our personal relationships? We meet and marry people who have a history of breaking every person's heart who has ever entrusted them with it. We later blame those same people for breaking our hearts. Sure, we ask questions, but we don't test the spirits like God told us to.

Intimate relationships are different. They first start off as intellectual since we have to get to know the people we plan to engage with. These relationships become more and more intimate (I'm not referring to sex or sexual favors) when we open up to them and they open up to us. Note: this doesn't mean that you should open up to everyone who opens their hearts to you or form intimate relationships with these people. Over the course of time, you'll notice that mature and Godly people who are called to your life are intentional as it relates to us. For example, I am oftentimes considered the "strong friend." Because of this, I tend to attract people who want and need counseling, and the only way they know to get it is by placing the wrong labels on the people they feel can be beneficial to them. Many people do this intentionally, meaning they have become somewhat manipulative, while others do this instinctively as a means of survival.

In short, every time you meet a person who wants intimate access to your heart, follow these steps:
1. **Pray about the person**. Don't give them intimate access until God confirms that He's sent them or they are mature enough to handle the roles and

responsibilities they are auditioning for. In this, don't open up to the person or allow the person to open up to you. Keep your relationship above the surface.

2. **Test the spirit.** You do this by examining the fruits that are growing in their lives. Which do you find in abundance: the works of the flesh or the fruits of the Spirit (see Galatians 5)? Act accordingly.

3. **Take your time.** Don't allow them to pressure or rush you into a relationship by mislabeling you.

4. **Ask questions.** Ask them about their former friends and lovers. Look for accountability. Do they take responsibility for their roles in their failed relationships or do they deflect the blame to others? If they don't take responsibility for their wrongs, they are immature, broken or both. This is what toxic relationships are made of.

5. **Establish, solidify and execute boundaries.** Most toxic and narcissistic people not only hate boundaries but they are incredibly impatient. They want to rush into relationships and they demand intimate access because they cannot handle intellectual access. This doesn't mean that they're not intelligent people, because many of them are; it means that they're not emotionally mature enough to handle farsightedness in relationships because they fear that their issues are better hidden from up close.

One of the systems I've created that's been incredibly
beneficial to me is something I call the Circle of Life. Look
at the drawing below.

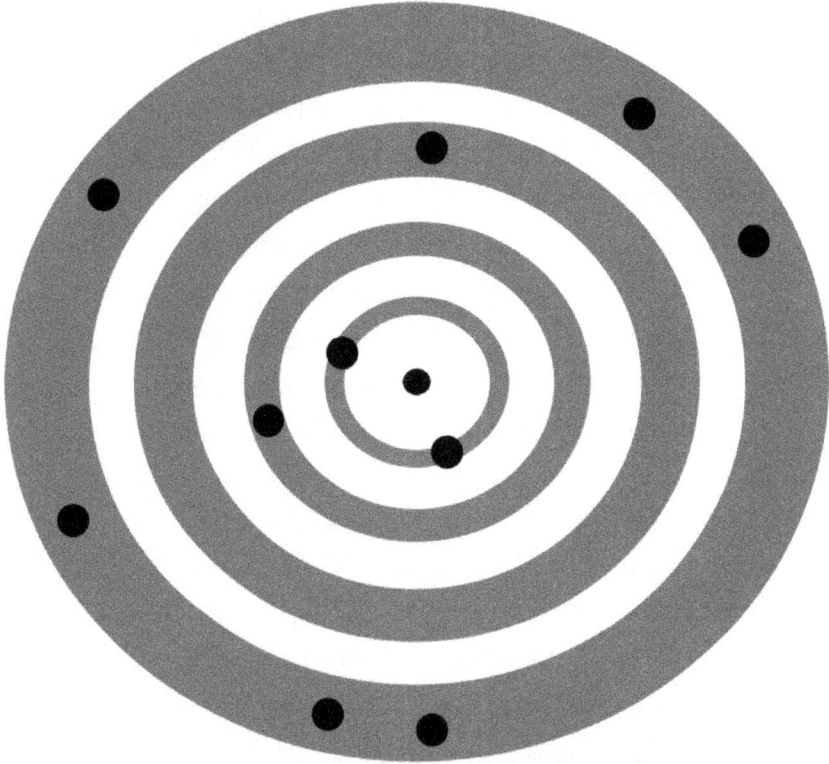

You'll notice that the drawing depicts a center (this
represents your heart), and around this center are circles.
Every dot on the circle represents a person. Everyone who
enters your life should start at the circle furthest away
from your heart. This is the intellectual space. Now, there
will be some people who get offended and walk away

whenever you don't allow them to rush into the most intimate places of your heart. If and when this happens, you can rest assured that they were not sent to you by God. They were likely toxic or maybe even narcissistic. Allow each person to show you what measure of access they can handle. For example, let's say that you meet a woman named Haley. Haley is both kind and patient. You get to know her more and more intellectually, and you notice that Haley is always checking up on you, she's always super friendly, and most of all, she pays close attention to the things you say to her. All the same, she doesn't attempt to rush you into a friendship. Over the course of time, you may move Haley to Circle 4. This gives her more intellectual access to you, but it may not give you more intellectual access to her. After all, this shouldn't be the goal. The goal is to see where she fits in your life and where you fit in her life. In this, you may find yourself going out to eat or hanging around Haley a little more. And within this space, you discover that she appears to be integral, intentional and purposeful. One day, you may just find yourself pulling her closer. Now, don't get me wrong. I'm not saying that she is auditioning for these parts in your life. I'm saying that you have to test the spirit from afar and allow her to show you how close she can be to your heart. Let's say that one day, Haley manages to move from Circle 4 to Circle 3, and then eventually to Circle 2. The same is true in her life. She moves you closer as well because she finds that you are amazing, integral and definitely an asset to have around her. But in Circle 2,

Haley starts to become somewhat offensive and short-tempered. She calls you all the time, but rarely answers your calls. This is typically a sign that Haley can't handle that level of access to you. It's also a sign that you may have mislabeled the relationship. It is possible that Haley may be a baby sister in Christ. In other words, she may serve as a mentee, which means that her assignment is to glean wisdom, knowledge and understanding from you. Then again, you may be her mentee. Either way, you have to give her the space that she needs to fully function in your life. So, you would have to usher her back to Circle 3. If she cannot handle that particular circle, you would move her to Circle 4. What does this look like? First and foremost, don't see this as a demotion; it's simply a repositioning. In this, you'd simply:

1. **Not avail yourself to her as often.** Each level gives the person a certain measure of access. People in Circle 5 will have far more access to you than the people in any other circle.

2. **Not open yourself up to her so intimately.** Don't tell her what is reserved for your intimate connections. (Note: this is why you need intimate connections! If you don't have them, you will share intimate details with your intellectual connections, and this will almost always prove to be detrimental to your mental, emotional and spiritual health).

3. **Not expect so much of her.** To whom much is given, much is required. When you place the right labels on relationships, there is less offense and

more results because you learn to examine and
respect everyone's capacity, maturity and what
they bring to the table.

4. **Not allow her to burden you with unrealistic
   expectations.** Every level of access has a certain
   measure of benefits; the same is true in the
   workplace, the marketplace and in relationships.

Again, this isn't a punishment or a demotion. It becomes a
punishment if you bring her close and then push her away
repeatedly in an attempt to tame or control her. That's a
form of emotional or relational witchcraft. Instead, you
should not be offended that she cannot function so closely
to you. Think about an aerosol can. It works great when it's
away from heat, but you can't place it too close to your
stove. The contents of the can are good and they help you
to accomplish certain tasks, but they are flammable. The
same is true for some people. For example, easily offended
people should never have intimate access to you. Proverbs
22:24-25 says it this way, "Make no friendship with an
angry man; and with a furious man thou shalt not go:
Lest thou learn his ways, and get a snare to thy soul." If
you give Haley the right roles in your life, and you assume
the right roles and responsibilities in her life, the two of
you may have some awesome times together and you may
build some great things together.

Lastly, please note that when seasons change, we often
have to move some people around in our lives, just as we
have to allow them to shift us so that we can fit into the

roles where we function the most. The key is to keep the offense out of it all and to try and understand why someone who was, for example, in Circle 5 is now in Circle 3. It's not always personal; oftentimes, it's spiritual. When you realize the intentionality of God and how He moves people around in our lives, you will have to do less healing, and this will allow you to function in your God-given assignment all the more.

Consumers vs. Producers

A consumer consumes; a producer produces. These are the most practical definitions. Fortune Magazine reported the following:

> "The top 0.01% richest individuals—the 520,000 people who have at least $19 million— now hold 11% of the world's wealth, up a full percentage point from 2020, the report found. Meanwhile, the share of global wealth owned by billionaires has grown from 1% in 1995 to 3% in 2021" (Source: Fortune.com/ World's richest people now own 11% of global wealth, marking the biggest leap in recent history/Nicole Goodkind).

Consumer (Oxford Languages):
- a person who purchases goods and services for personal use.
- a person or thing that eats or uses something.

Producer (Oxford Languages):
- a person, company, or country that makes, grows, or supplies goods or commodities for sale.
- a person or thing that makes or causes something.

In short, a consumer takes or consumes; a producer gives or produces.

The following information was taken from Oberlo.com:

"Here's a summary of the Entrepreneur statistics you need to know in 2022:

1. There are 582 million entrepreneurs in the world (MARKINBLOG, 2020).
2. Nearly 5.4 million new businesses were started in the US in 2021 (Census, 2022).
3. As of 2020, there were 274 million female entrepreneurs worldwide (GEM Consortium, 2021).
4. More than six in ten (63 percent) of US small businesses were profitable in 2020 (Guidant Financial, 2021).
5. 72 percent of US businesses owned by African Americans are profitable (Guidant Financial, 2020).
6. More than half of the new businesses started in the US over the past decade are minority-owned (SBC, 2020).
7. The number of people wanting to start their own business because of their dissatisfaction with corporate America grew 27 percent this year (Guidant Financial, 2020).
8. In 2018, 15.6 percent of all US adults were entrepreneurs (Entrepreneurship.babson.edu, 2019).
9. 67.7 percent of the world's wealthiest individuals (with a net worth of at least $30 million) are self-made (CNBC, 2019).
10. Nearly one in five (18.7 percent) of businesses worldwide takes on the form of family entrepreneurship in one way or another (GEM Consortium, 2019).

Source: Oberlo.com/Ten Entrepreneur Statistics That You Need to Know in 2022/Ying Lin)

I shared these articles to illustrate a point, and that is—the majority of people on the face of this planet are consumers. Entrepreneurs are solutionists and, of course, there are solutionists out there who aren't necessarily entrepreneurs (ex: politicians, doctors, lawyers, etc.). Nevertheless, the large majority of the world's wealth is found in the bank accounts of entrepreneurs. What's a notable difference between a consumer and a producer? Consumers complain about the problems they come face-to-face with and consumers avoid problems at all costs. Producers see problems as opportunities, therefore, producers tend to look for problems. Some will even create problems to solve. The beauty industry is renowned for this. They partner with the mass media to create beauty standards, and then they market products (mostly to women) to help them reach those standards. •

Why are we discussing consumers and producers? My goal is to give you language so that you can understand the next few chapters of this book. You may be a producer, and while you may not be a business owner, you are a problem-solver. Consequently, you are seen as the strong friend; this is the person who everyone turns to when times get tough. This is also the individual who can't seem to find a shoulder to cry on whenever he or she is in the midst of a storm. The majority of people on the face of this planet are consumers or, better yet, takers. And because of this, producers are oftentimes taken advantage of. All the same, a lot of people who fall into this category are introverts, or they become introverted over the course of time. This is why social interactions can be draining to them. They are oftentimes seen as problem-solvers, therefore, people flock to them for answers. And even when they are in the midst of people but standing somewhere off to themselves, introverts, by default, oftentimes see problems that others don't seem to notice. This causes them to:

1. Question what they've witnessed.
2. Question why no one else sees what they see.
3. To mentally draft solutions to the problems; solutions that they rarely try to implement. This causes creative constipation (more on this later).
4. Try and pretend that there is no problem so that they don't draw attention to themselves.
5. Further distance themselves from people they deem to be trouble-makers, thus, further isolating themselves from the world.

Again, producers are oftentimes introverts and many of them are ambiverts. They are wired this way because they need time to themselves to hear from God and to produce. It goes without saying that many would-be producers never produce any good thing because they are oftentimes distracted by consumers (platonic, romantic, familial).

If you are a consumer, you have to understand why some of your strongest or wisest friends need a break away from you from time to time. After all, consumers:

1. Complain about problems.

2. Refuse to solve problems, but instead, they often choose to stay in the midst of the very things and people they complain about the most.

3. Give their energy (virtue) to those problems, and when they are drained from doing so, they reach out to solutionists (producers) to refuel themselves. This is why they will complain nonstop about an issue or a set of issues, and then finalize their phone calls with, "Thank you so much for hearing me out! I just needed to vent, but I feel so much better now!" What just happened is they made an exchange. They transferred the weight of their frustrations to the solutionists and took the solutionists peace away. So, when they hang up the phone, they feel better, but the solutionists often feel drained.

4. They are rarely grateful. Consider the ten lepers who Jesus healed. Luke 17:11-19 tells the story. "And it came to pass, as he went to Jerusalem, that he passed through the midst of Samaria and Galilee. And as he entered into a certain village, there met him ten men that were lepers, which stood afar off: And they lifted up their voices, and said, Jesus, Master, have mercy on us. And when he saw them, he said unto them, Go shew yourselves unto the priests. And it came to pass, that, as they went, they were cleansed. And one of them, when he saw that he was healed, turned back, and with a loud voice glorified God, and fell down on his face at

his feet, giving him thanks: and he was a Samaritan. And Jesus answering said, Were there not ten cleansed? But where are the nine? There are not found that returned to give glory to God, save this stranger. And he said unto him, Arise, go thy way: thy faith hath made thee whole."

The consumer/producer tag is the first set of labels you need to familiarize yourself with because every other label we discuss in this book will fall under these two categories. The first assignment is to identify who you are to everyone who plays a role in your life and to identify who those people are to you. Are you a consumer or producer? In which relationships do you play the role of the producer/problem-solver, and in which relationships do you play the role of the consumer? If you say that you play both roles in your relationships, chances are, you are a consumer in most, if not all of those relationships. Why do I say this? Because consumers don't like to be referred to as consumers, so to avoid this tag/label, they remind themselves of the moments and times when they helped to solve a problem or a set of problems in their relationships. The problem with this is—consumers do solve problems, but the scale is not balanced! An example that I like to use to help people to locate where they are is this: Imagine that you are an adult and one of your neighbors is a four-year old child. You have a job, you're obviously a lot more mature than the child and you're relatively independent. You often encounter this four-year old little boy whenever you return home from work and he's always standing outside playing with his toys. And every time he sees you, he asks for money or candy, and most of the time, you tell him no. Whenever you say no to him, he crosses his arms, pouts and shouts, "I don't want to be your friend anymore!" This is typical four-year old behavior; right? It's nothing too alarming! But one day, you return home to see him playing with his toy helicopter. You get out of the car holding a bag, and in this bag, you have a large bag of potato chips and a few groceries. The little boy drops his helicopter and rushes over to you. "Can I have some?" he asks, eyeing the bag of chips sticking out of your bag. You think about it and smile. "Sure, you can have the whole bag." The little boy shouts for joy, hugs you and then grabs the bag of chips, pulling it from your bag before running back to where he had been playing initially. Ten minutes later, you have an epitome. You'd purchased those chips because you were hungry and hadn't felt like cooking. Plus, you need to take your medication. So, you head out the door with a small plate in your hand, and since you've given him a large back of chips, it seems reasonable for you to ask for a few of them back. Nevertheless, the little boy's countenance changes when he sees the plate. He shoves the chips in his mouth as he kicks his legs playfully while sitting on a lawn chair. "Hey Junior, can I have a handful of chips?" you ask. Junior pouts. "No!" he shouts, turning his body away from you as if he's trying to protect his chips. "Junior, please," you say with a soft voice. "I need to take my medicine." Junior continues to frown, but he eventually turns around and places a few chips on your plate. What did Junior just do? He gave you back a percentage of what once belonged to you. This is what demons do and this is what people do! What I mean by this is—if you are a consumer, you've taken a lot of another person's time and/or resources. Understand this—once a person gives you "their time," it becomes your time because they are transferring it to you. And, of course, whatever resources they share with you become yours if they hand it over without saying that it's a loan. The minute you give them some of your time and/or resources, you are simply returning a percentage of what they've given you. In other words, the scales aren't balanced in consumer/producer relationships because the producer often gives 75–99 percent more than what he or she receives from the consumer. The consumer gives a little as well, but the scales are tilted in the consumer's favor, not the producer's. In order for you to label a relationship, for example, a friendship, it has to be a just weight, meaning it has to be balanced. Now, understand this—friendships are not always balanced; they shift from season to season. In one season, your friend may be the producer and you may be the consumer because you may be in a series of storms, and in the next season, the roles may reverse. We determine who our friends are once we've seen these roles reverse a few times and we're able to locate the pattern. If you are always there for your friends when they need you, but the moment you need them, they are chronically unavailable, you don't have a friendship with them. You may be their mentor; then again, they could potentially be opportunists. This is what I mean when I say anyone who proudly shouts that they play both roles are typically consumers because producers only remember what they'd done for their friends if the scales are imbalanced! Going back to the little boy with the bag of chips, if someone were to say to him, "You're not being nice! That man (or woman) gave you a big bag of chips, and you were acting stingy when he/she asked for a handful of those chips," the little boy would likely shout, "I gave him some chips!" After this, he'd pout. Because of his immaturity, this would lead him to believe that he's fair-minded and even justified in how he'd treated you. This is how consumers think as well. It's hard for a consumer to conceptualize the fact that he or she falls under the category of a taker. Look at it this way. There are two guys in this story: Ralph and Jacob.

- Ralph has $4.5 million in his bank account.
- Jacob has $4,500 in his bank account.

Ralph and Jacob are friends. Christmas comes around, and both men decide to buy Christmas gifts for one another.

- Jacob buys Ralph a watch valued at $100.
- Ralph buys Jacob a pair of shoes valued at $150.

The men exchange gifts on Christmas Eve. Ralph looks at the watch and thanks his friend for the gift. Jacob, on the other hand, looks at the shoes and immediately remembers seeing them at the mall. While he likes those shoes and definitely wanted a pair, deep down in his heart, he feels somewhat disappointed. Ralph notices Jacob's attempt to look happy, but he knows that something is wrong, so he asks his friend, "Hey, are you okay?" Jacob forces a smile on his face and says, "Yeah, thanks. I love the shoes." After the two men part ways, Jacob calls his other friend, Tony. He tells Tony about his dilemma. He says, "This man is worth over four million dollars! I can't believe he's so cheap! He bought me a pair of shoes that costs $150! Now get this—I know that the gift I bought him was only a hundred bucks, but that's because I don't have a lot of money to spare, but this dude is worth well over four million dollars!" What's happening here? Relationships like these fairly work because the person who has less typically will expect more. The Bible confirms this in Luke 12:48, which reads, "For unto whomsoever much is given, of him shall be much required: and to whom men have committed much, of him they will ask the more." Is Jacob a bad guy? No, he's acting his (financial) age. This may sound offensive until you find yourself serving as the producer in a relationship with someone who believes that you should give more of your time and resources simply because you have more than they have. This makes me think of a former friend of mine who was always "down on her luck." She would often spoke reproachfully about the people who attempted to help her because she always felt like they weren't doing enough. Simply put, she felt entitled to their homes when she had nowhere to stay, entitled to their time when she didn't have anything to do, and entitled to their resources when she had very little to contribute. And she would always justify her entitlement with, "They know my situation!" The problem with this mentality is that consumers rarely stop being consumers, meaning her situation wasn't going to change—ever—that is unless she allowed God to change her mind! So, she took more than she gave; she said "thank you" more than she said, "you're welcome," and she kept a record of the times when she'd helped another person. And because she wasn't used to giving to others, she valued the little she did for others over the major sacrifices they'd made on her behalf. Whenever the people who were attempting to help her pointed out her ways, she would say, "I didn't ask you to do all that." Over the course of time, everyone that she leaned on for support and help stopped enabling her, and this would only seem to upset her all the more. She felt wronged, but she hadn't been mishandled in any way. Of course, I pointed this out to her, but she couldn't seem to fathom what I was talking about. I think about some of my relatives who reasoned this way. They were oftentimes upset with every other relative who had dared to break the curse of poverty and reach for their goals in life. They would oftentimes frown whenever they heard these relatives' names and say:

- "Why? She hasn't done anything for me!"
- "She thinks she's better than everyone!"
- "What goes up must come down!"
- "One day, somebody's gonna knock her off her high horse!"

This is entitlement at its best! This is why consumers hang around consumers, and producers surround themselves with other productive people! And because there aren't that many producers on the face of this planet, producers are known to walk alone and build alone; that is until they come in contact with other producers who are consistent, integral and purpose-driven.

Again, the purpose of this particular chapter is to prime or prepare you for the rest of what you're about to read. But before you move on, be sure to create a list of the people in your life, and determine whether or not those people are producers or consumers. Also, determine what roles you play in their lives versus what roles they play in your life. Once you have created these lists, you will be ready to move to the next chapter.

UNDERSTANDING VOIDS

What do you think of when you hear the word "void"? Let's look at a few definitions for this word. Please note that the following definitions were taken from Oxford Languages.

Void:

1. completely empty (adjective).
2. a completely empty space (noun).
3. declare that (something) is not valid or legally binding (verb).

In short, the word "void" means:

1. Hollow.
2. Without light.
3. Without form.

Genesis 1:1-2 reads, "In the beginning God created the heaven and the earth. And the earth was without form, and void; and darkness was upon the face of the deep. And the Spirit of God moved upon the face of the waters." Notice that the Earth was without form and void; this means that the Earth had no shape because it had no purpose. All the same, it was empty; this is what it means to be void. How did God respond? Genesis 1:3 answers this question; it reads, "And God said, Let there be light: and there was light." Let's look at another scripture; let's look at 1 John 1:5, which reads, "This then is the message which we have heard of him, and declare unto you, that God is light, and in him is no darkness at all." In summary, without God's presence, the Earth was without form and void; with God's presence, the Earth began to be filled with purpose. Now, think of yourself and every human being who has ever walked the face of this Earth as little earths. We were all formed by God, just as the Earth was, but sin deformed us; this is why we have to be transformed by the renewing of our minds. How are we transformed? Through information, and by information, I mean the Word of God and every word that proceeds from His mouth.

Voids are like black holes in the soul; these are spots that are empty of light, and by light, please understand that biblically speaking, light represents revelation or a revealing. These holes are often found in our hearts. It simply means the absence of knowledge, understanding or wisdom, and when these three are not in a space, God won't be in that space. Our soul is comprised of our mind, will and emotions. When the Bible speaks of the mind, it is referencing the heart. Again, this is the part of us that we are supposed to guard. Voids are typically found in the heart; they are brought on by:
1. Lack of information.
2. Lack of affirmation.
3. Trauma.

We are multidimensional creatures; we have, for example,

our parental states, our sibling states, our financial states, our platonic (friendly) states, our romantic states, our mental states and the list goes on. Each of these states has to be surrendered and submitted to God. Anytime there is a state that is absent of light or revelation, that state will be without form and void, meaning it will be filled with voids. Again, voids are like black holes in the soul; they have a strong gravitational pull; we call this pull "attraction." This means that who we find ourselves drawn to are often a reflection of our voids, meaning the content of our hearts reveals the intent of our hearts. Obviously, we are supposed to give God His seat and let Him heal us in those areas, but believe it or not, wherever you have an abundance of voids, you will find yourself looking for void-fillers outside of God.

Next, remember that Satan is the prince of darkness. What do you find in voids? Emptiness, of course. And where there is emptiness and no light, there will be darkness. This means that demons hide in voids, after all, they cannot bear the presence of light. This is why I often educate people who seek deliverance with these words— deliverance casts the demons out of the darkness, but it does not turn the lights on. Matthew 12:43-45 states, "When an unclean spirit goes out of a man, he goes through dry places, seeking rest, and finds none. Then he says, 'I will return to my house from which I came.' And when he comes, he finds it empty, swept, and put in order. Then he goes and takes with him seven other spirits more wicked than himself, and they enter and dwell there; and the last state of that man is worse than the first. So shall it also be with this wicked generation." Notice where the unclean spirit finds rest. It finds rest in a soul that is empty; again, the word "empty" means "void." Some theologians theorize that the darkness that was upon the face of the deep were demonic spirits, after all, when Satan and his angels were cast out of Heaven, they were cast into the Earth. Could it be that the Earth was a temporary holding center for devils, and when God sent man into the Earth, man was operating as an apostolic unit, designed to recover the Earth by simply growing the garden of God? Either way, sin entered man, and with sin came the absence of God. And now that Jesus has reconciled us to the Father, we must understand that we have to submit to God the entirety of our beings. This is what it means to love Him with all of our hearts. In other words, we can't be double-minded. If we want to walk in our Kingdom authority and tap into our Godly inheritance, we have to allow God to occupy every state of our hearts. We have to fill ourselves with His Word; we must build our faith and then apply it. We must also submit ourselves to God and resist the devil; this, according to James 4:7, would cause the devil to flee from us.

Understand this—our attractions to people are often centered around our voids. For example, a young woman whose father was absent from her life may find herself attracted to men who are significantly older than herself.

In this, she may look for men to fill that room in the parental state called the father room. The problem with this is—she will likely find herself attracted to broken older men who are hellbent on controlling women. Remember, voids have a strong gravitational pull called attraction. This is why you have a "type." Your type is centered around your voids, and again, demons hide in voids. This is why I tell people that we can cast demons out of the voids, but we can't cast the darkness out. God is Light; He is Revelation. He is His Word, and we need His Word to illuminate those empty spaces.

What does all of this mean? Matthew 6:33 states, "But seek ye first the kingdom of God, and his righteousness; and all these things shall be added unto you." Notice that this scripture deals with order. In this, God tells us to seek His Kingdom <u>first</u>, along with His righteousness. In other words, our assignment is to seek His Word and His will; that is, to prioritize Him above everything and everyone else. If a man or a woman gets into one of those states before we allow God in them, those people will be overwhelmed and consumed by whatever it is that's been lodging in those states, whether it's false doctrine or a bunch of demons. All the same, please note that there is a such thing as a familiar spirit. This particular class of demons typically migrate from one generation to the other, wreaking havoc and chaos in every state that they're in. And whenever you come across one of these spirits, you may feel extremely comfortable with the person hosting them because there is a sense of familiarity present. For example, have you ever met a person of the opposite sex who, after a few days, you felt incredibly comfortable with? You felt like you'd known the person a lot longer; right? This is your discernment kicking in, but when you're broken, you won't understand that you're encountering or rebuilding a relationship with an unclean spirit and that this particular demon has patterns.

To increase in relational intelligence or acuity, we must first seek the Kingdom of God and we must also work towards getting all of our voids filled with the Word of God. Remember, if God isn't in that state of your heart, the enemy will send some of his workers to inhabit that area. From there, they will build a siege wall, often referred to as a stronghold. According to Oxford Languages, a stronghold is:

1. a place that has been fortified so as to protect it against attack.
2. a place where a particular cause or belief is strongly defended or upheld.

In this, the enemy will try to protect your heart from the truth; this way, he can keep you under his control. And when the heart is filled with voids and lies, you will find yourself attracted to liars, rebels and people who don't mind being worshiped (narcissists). All the same, be mindful of this fact—people with voids will always be attracted to you when you are filled with voids and when you've been made whole. To be made whole is to be filled with God and healed in every state of your being. And to identify broken souls, you must understand the labels that they use and how to avoid being sucked into a relationship, be it platonic or romantic, that's both unhealthy and toxic. Understand this—every time you endure another trauma from up close (think intimate relationship), that trauma serves like a wrecking ball; it impacts your soul all the more. This impact will continue until it creates a hole in another state. For example, your financial state borders your mental state. So, if the enemy can attack your finances repeatedly, he can also affect your mental health and vice versa. Over the course of time, you may find yourself trying to repair the damage done to your finances by getting romantically involved with someone who's more stable financially. Believe it or not, this behavior is common! And while in that relationship, you may deal with mental and emotional abuse. Do you see how demons used the wrecking ball of trauma to create a hole between your financial state and your mental state? From there, they will continue to advance into other states unless addressed through obedience, the Word of God and the ministry of deliverance. But you can do as God did. When He saw that the Earth was void and without form, He said, "Let there be light!" Again, He is Light! So, the correct and most effective way to address voids is through studying the Word of God, and not just by reading your Bible, but by:

1. Showing up at church on Sundays.
2. Showing up to Bible Study during the midweek.

3. Watching live lessons from leaders who have been anointed by God to preach the gospel.

4. Buying and studying good and Godly books, especially books on subjects that you are void of revelation in.

5. Getting wise counsel. Proverbs 11:14 reads, "Where no counsel is, the people fall: but in the multitude of counselors there is safety."

6. Surrounding yourself with God-fearing people who are not double-minded (see Matthew 6:22, James 1:8).

7. Get therapy and lots of it! Wise counsel deals with your future, but therapy deals with the past because your past does affect your present and it impacts your future. So yes, you need both wise counsel and therapy!

8. Through prayer. God loves honesty. For example, whenever you find yourself in the midst of a storm, pray this prayer, "God, please give me the wisdom from the storm and take away everything else that is harmful or is not beneficial to me. I forgive everyone who's hurt me, and I still say yes to whatever you want to do in my life. I am your yielded vessel. Silence the enemy on my behalf, in Jesus' name."

9. By ministering to others. You'd be amazed at how much revelation you've stored in your heart; this revelation will only come out when you're edifying and encouraging someone else. All the same, we

often have faith for others, but not for ourselves, and wherever there is faith, there will also be revelation. This is why encouraging or edifying someone else often sets the tone for God to encourage and edify us.

10. By putting God first! Shallowness, hollowness or emptiness is oftentimes the product of selfishness.

INTIMATE SPACES

The measure of access a person has to your house represents the level or measure of access that he or she has to your heart. For example, think of the people in your life.

1. Who has access to your kitchen?
2. Who can freely open your refrigerator?
3. Who have you invited into your bedroom?
4. Who can freely roam your home?

Most people that you allow in your house will be restricted to your living room. And while your home is your intimate space, there are degrees or levels of intimacy within your home. Imagine inviting one of your co-workers to your house for the first time. Now, imagine that the co-worker in question walks through your door, greets you and says, "What do y'all have to eat over here?" She then makes her way out of your living room and starts heading towards your kitchen, asking "Is the kitchen this way?" What would you do? Chances are, you would follow her; you'd be confused, offended and you'd be trying to figure out which response would be the proper one. How would you feel if she opened your refrigerator and started moving things around, talking about, "Do you have anything sweet to eat in here?" Should you be confrontational? Should you be rude? Or should you avoid offending her altogether? If you're like most people, you'd elect to offend her, but you'd try to keep from elevating your voice. You'd likely say, "What are you doing? Are you okay? Hey sis, this is not okay." Why would you respond this way? Because you'd be trying to let her know that she doesn't have the right to invite herself into the intimate spaces of your home. You'd be communicating with her that she has crossed some boundaries and you are not pleased with her behavior.

We talked about Circles 1–5, so I want you to liken them to your house. Imagine that:

1. **Circle 5** is your communal space; this is an intellectual zone or space. This is where you meet people. It represents the most distant form of intellectual access; this means that the person has a measure of personal access to you, but the two of you don't really know one another. This is where you meet; this is where you commune. If the person is decent, you'd likely invite him or her into Circle 4.

2. **Circle 4** is your phone number. Now, just because someone has your phone number doesn't automatically mean that the person is in Circle 4. Your phone number is simply an invitation to this circle IF you have been communicating with the person in the communal space that you two share, and if you've shared a certain amount of intimate information and vice versa. If you have never communicated with the person, on the other hand, and the individual asks for your phone number, the person will enter into Circle 5 when he or she calls you. Circle 4 is your way of giving a person permission to be in constant contact with you,

whether this frequency looks like a month, a few months, weeks or days.

3. **Circle 3** is your living room. This space can be both intimate and intellectual. For example, you may open the door for a neighbor you don't personally know if she asks to borrow something from you. By allowing her into your home, you are expressing a certain level of trust, but chances are, you wouldn't invite her to take a seat or ask if she wants something to drink.

4. **Circle 2** is your kitchen. While this is an intimate space, you would likely invite people into this space that you trust and have built a measure of rapport with.

5. **Circle 1** is your bedroom. This is the most intimate space in the house, only reserved for people who have the most intimate connection with you; this includes your spouse, your parents and your closest friends.

Now, let's look at what this represents with the heart.

1. **Circle 5** are the people you see whenever you go to church, work, school or wherever you gather. These are the people that you're on good terms with, but you don't personally know one another. You may find yourself greeting these people or even having a few conversations here and there, but outside of the communal space, you don't personally know them.

2. **Circle 4** are the people you've exchanged phone numbers with, and you may have eaten out with

them a time or two. These people have more personal access to you, even though they are in your intellectual circle. They don't necessarily know you outside of what you've shared with them, but they are oftentimes getting to know you. Then again, these can be people who were once in Circles 1, 2 or 3 who intimately know the person you once were but can't relate to who you've become.

3. **Circle 3** are the folks you've invited to your home, a birthday party or maybe even your wedding. While they are still in your intellectual circle, you may have labeled them as friends (standard or distant), even though they aren't necessarily your close friends and you don't speak with them over the phone a lot. Then again, you may have labeled them as confidants, or you may be vetting them to become friends.

4. **Circle 2** are people who are in your intimate circle; these are the people you consider to be friends, even though they aren't necessarily your best friends or closest friends. The people in this circle are people you may find yourself speaking with occasionally, and then there are some seasons where you may find yourself speaking with them frequently. Whenever you speak with them, you will notice that you are very open with them as it relates to your life, but in those times when you have not spoken in a while, you will likely spend hours updating them about your life and vice versa. And while you will likely have a great deal of trust for the people in this particular circle, you will find

that you don't always tell them every intimate detail about your life; this is often because they need context, meaning they need to understand the thoughts and circumstances that led up to some of the decisions you've made.

5. **Circle 1** is your most intimate space. These are the people you trust with the most intimate details of your life. These are oftentimes the people you may find yourself listing as references on your job applications and as emergency contacts at your jobs and at the hospitals. These people know almost all there is to know about you. Most of the people in this circle are people you speak with every single day or every week. Then again, some of them are people you speak with once a month or every few months because of their job, family or school schedules. Nevertheless, what makes them stand out from Circle 2 is that you trust them with your life.

Understand that this circle moves clockwise and counterclockwise, meaning there are people moving outward, just as there are people moving inward. Of course, the people moving outward are getting further away from you, and the people moving inward are getting closer to you. Whenever this movement ceases, it typically means that you are locked in a season because of comfort, fear, trauma or sin, or you have reached your love capacity. In short, your capacity to love others has everything to do with how much love you've extended to others through selflessness (listening to others, sacrificing for others, helping others and supporting others). If you have spent a great deal of time being selfish, meaning you've chosen to be a Consumer in your relationships and not a Producer, your capacity to love others will be extremely limited. This would cause you to become intolerant of others, thus causing the tornado effect of the circle to move at a greater speed counterclockwise than it does clockwise. This means that you may move people close to your heart at an accelerated rate, but those people move away from your heart at an even greater rate once they discover that the scales are tilted in your favor, not theirs. In other words, when they discover that you are taking more than you are giving, most people will begin the process of distancing themselves from you or exiting your life altogether. All the same, if this circle is moving too fast, it could only mean:

1. You're a narcissist or you are relatively narcissistic. Narcissists move fast in relationships so that they can get access to what the world of psychology refers to as narcissistic supply. Narcissistic supply refers to the constant supply of attention and admiration that narcissists require to function in everyday life.

2. You have some pretty sizable voids. Remember that voids are like black holes; they have a vacuum effect called attraction, and this effect causes people to become somewhat desperate. In other words, they use people as void-fillers; that is until they discover that each individual they bring into their lives is incapable of satisfying them. But, rather than taking accountability and getting the healing they

need, most people with sizable voids see themselves as victims; this causes them to deal with perpetual disappointment, and this disappointment causes them to discard familiar people, all the while rushing new people into their intimate spaces.

3. You need deliverance. Demons are soul consumers, and they have the appetite of fire; this means that they are never and can never be satisfied.

Your intimate space can be found in your heart; this is what the Bible told you to guard. Most people don't know what it means to guard their hearts; they think that the scripture is simply telling them to not fall in love too quickly or to avoid toxic people, and while this is true, the real questions are—how do you stop yourself from falling in love too fast and how do you avoid toxic people? The answer has been under our noses this whole time! Simply put, guard information that is considered to be sensitive; this is information that you wouldn't share with the world at large. You see, every circle of people has a certain measure of access to your heart; this means that they have access to a certain level of information. You probably wouldn't tell your secrets to people in Circle 5 because you don't know what they are going to do with that information. Nevertheless, you likely know who the people in Circle 1 communicate with the most, and you know their character. We've all made the mistake of giving out way too much information to people who were not in our intimate circles. This typically happens whenever we find ourselves alone with them, and for one reason or another, we felt compelled to share some of our most intimate life stories with them. This is a common occurrence for people who have broken hearts; brokenhearted people rarely guard their hearts because they are looking for ways to make the pain stop. This is why it is imperative that we surround ourselves with wise counsel; these are God-fearing people who we can reach out to whenever we find ourselves in the midst of a storm. People who don't have wise counselors will talk to anyone who's willing to listen. Think about rebound relationships. The following information was taken from MyTherapist.com:

> "An empirical research study conducted by Brumbaugh and Fraley defines a rebound relationship as 'A relationship initiated shortly after a romantic breakup – before the feelings about the former relationship have been resolved.'
> Simply stated, a rebound relationship is one that isn't expected to last or grow beyond its current state. In most cases of rebound relationships, one partner is clear that the relationship isn't ever going to go anywhere – yet they participate in the relationship anyway to avoid feeling the pain of grief and loss from their recent breakup" (Source: My Therapist/The Rebound Relationship: Deep Dive).

We all need therapy because, according to Job 14:1, "Man that is born of a woman is of few days, and full of trouble." Get this—1 Peter 5:8 says, "Be sober, be vigilant; because your adversary the devil, as a roaring lion, walketh about, seeking whom he may devour." The word "may" is a permissive word; it suggests that Satan cannot devour everyone. Who then can he devour? The Greek word for "devour" is "katesthió," and according to Strong's Accordance, it means "to eat up." Another word for the phrase "eat up" is "consume." Another word for "consume" is "overwhelm" or "to fully encompass." Isaiah 59:19 reads, "So shall they fear the name of the LORD from the west, and his glory from the rising of the sun. When the enemy shall come in like a flood, the Spirit of the LORD shall lift up a standard against him." What does a flood do? It consumes whatever it touches by encompassing that thing or that person. In short, we all need therapy because we are always dealing with heartache, disappointment and rejection. And believe it or not, we seek out therapy every day of our lives. The problem is that we don't always look for therapists; we often pacify our voids with:

1. **Retail Therapy** (We spend money on the things that make us feel better about ourselves or things that distract us from our current states).
2. **Romantic Relationships** (We use people to fill the voids created by other people).
3. **Friendships** (We tell our friends everything in hopes that they can help us to figure out our next moves).
4. **Drugs and Alcohol** (While these toxins are detrimental to our mental health and our existence as a whole, they oftentimes provide temporary relief from the stresses that we face).

This is to say BEWARE! There are a LOT of hurting people out there who will readily use you to make themselves feel better. This is called objectification. According to Good

Therapy, "Objectification involves viewing and/or treating a person as an object, devoid of thought or feeling." The point is—when a person enters your life:

1. Keep that person in Circle 5 and let that person earn a spot in every circle; don't invite him or her into your intimate space without the individual proving himself or herself to be mature enough to have that level of access to you.

2. Always ensure that the person isn't using you as a replacement for another person. What I've discovered in my dealings with people is this—people who live in the past can't seem to stop talking about the past, so anyone they engage with in the present is simply an object to help them cope with their pasts. Pay attention to the direction of a person's conversation. If the future for that person is a response to his or her past, don't entertain the individual or, at minimum, keep that person in Circle 5. An example of this is when a person wants to be successful to hurt, prove themselves to or humiliate someone who has rejected, betrayed or hurt them in the past, that person should not be in your intimate circle.

3. Rebound relationships don't always happen immediately after a breakup. Most relationships today are rebound relationships. Whenever you don't end your conversation with your past, you will continue that conversation in your present. The faces of the people that you talk to will change, but the conversation will remain the same.

4. Any person who moves fast in relationships is both toxic and traumatized, regardless of whether the person acknowledges this or not. Don't allow anyone to rush out of your intellectual space and into your intimate space.

5. People who try to use other people to heal their hurts often hurt people. This vicious cycle doesn't end until someone who's gotten sucked into this tornado stops looking for a boyfriend/girlfriend and starts looking for a therapist.

And remember—always treat your relationships like you treat your house. Never allow people to come into intimate spaces without them first earning the right to be there. Lastly, never allow people to demand a measure of trust that they have not earned! Trust is built, not given! When someone is in Circle 5, that person is in the process of building trust with you; if that person demands access to more trust than he or she has earned, that person is toxic. This is why you should never allow people to rush into your intimate circle. Soul ties often become nooses when they are rushed into.

Intellectual Spaces

Believe it or not, your intellectual space is almost as important as your intimate space. This is why you shouldn't treat it like a trashcan. In other words, don't toss people you consider to be toxic into this space because any measure of access to your heart can prove to be fatal in more ways than one. Your intellectual space should be reserved for:

1. People you want to maintain relationships with who are too immature to be in your intimate space.
2. People you have no choice but to remain connected to (ex: co-parents, co-workers, co-laborers).
3. People you are getting to know.

As I mentioned in the previous chapter, your relational circle moves like a tornado, whereas some people should be spiraling out of your life, while others are increasing in your life. All the same, it is vital for you to know that some people won't move, for example, from Circle 1 to Circle 5 before exiting your life. You will likely come in contact with people you will have to completely remove from your life altogether the moment you discover that they are working against God's plan for your life. This is because having them too close could not only cause you a great deal of trauma, but it can cause delays in your life. Your mind works overtime to keep you sane. It does this by storing your traumas in the unconscious realm of the mind. The following information was taken from Very Well Mind:

"In Sigmund Freud's psychoanalytic theory of personality, the unconscious mind is defined as a reservoir of feelings, thoughts, urges, and memories that are outside of conscious awareness. Within this understanding, most of the contents of the unconscious are considered unacceptable or unpleasant, such as feelings of pain, anxiety, or conflict. Freud believed that the unconscious continues to influence behavior even though people are unaware of these underlying influences" (Source: VeryWellMind.com/What is the Unconscious?/Kendra Cherry).

If your mind, which is biblically referred to as your heart, works overtime to protect you from trauma, you have to work twice as hard to protect it. "Above all else, guard your heart, for everything you do flows from it" (Proverbs 4:23). What I've discovered in my dealings with people is that a large number of westerners simply don't know what it means to guard their hearts. Consequently, we are a broken nation. The problem isn't that there are evil people in this world; the problem is that we tolerate them and we allow them into our intimate spaces. We often do this because we think that we can change people who refuse to change for God. Believers pray for discernment all the time, but they rarely tap into it. Discernment isn't just a keen or supernatural ability to differentiate a good person from an evil one, after all, the Bible tells us that we will know them by their fruits (see Matthew 7:15-20). This means that we have the following responsibilities:

1. To know the difference between good fruits (the fruits of the Spirit) versus evil fruits (the works of the flesh and the wiles of the devil).
2. To examine the fruits of everyone who auditions for a role or a position in our lives.
3. To cut off or disassociate ourselves from anyone who does not bear good fruit.
4. To cast down the imaginations that would seduce us into believing that we can change broken people.

Don't get me wrong. I'm not saying that we shouldn't evangelize, after all, winning souls for Christ is our main objective. What I am saying is this—we shouldn't be sleeping with our assignments or partnering with people who have not partnered with God. And understand this—the more broken and immature a person is, the more passionate and/or desperate that person will be to get out of your intellectual circle and into your intimate circle! Good, healthy people take their time because they know their worth; they know they bring a lot to the table, and they reason this way—if you don't want to be a part of their lives, it is your loss, not theirs. Broken and unhealthy people reason differently. They rush to form bonds with anyone and everyone they deem to be a cure, a solution, an asset or a remedy for whatever problems they are facing, whether that problem is loneliness, poverty, trauma, debt, fear or addiction. In other words, broken people are often in survival mode. They romanticize what it would be like to be close to certain people, promising themselves that they'd be great friends or great assets to that person's life, not taking into accountability their relational records. I immediately think about this young lady who was so determined to be a part of my intimate space that she would call me every single day. She would tell me about her struggles, in essence giving me something to help her fix. The goal behind this behavior is to tap into what I call the fixer's function, especially those of us who are Solutionists/Producers. I didn't let her get too close, but I did allow her in Circle 3. From there, she began to steal from me, proving to me once and for all just how desperate a person in survival mode can be. All the same, women tend to be fixers, whereas men tend to be protectors. In other words, most women have a very sensitive trigger on their fixer's function. Broken people play damsels in distress whenever they come in contact with fixers, just as they play the role of a heroine whenever they come in contact with someone who needs fixing. But what is the fixer's function? In short, it is comprised of three elements:

1. Our need to help others.
2. Our ability to help others.
3. Our passion for helping others.

Think about one of your toxic exes (if you have any). Why did you tolerate that particular ex for so long? Chances are, you saw an area of deficiency in that person's life and you justified his or her behavior by highlighting that deficiency. You then attempted to fix that particular ex, and anytime you concluded that your ex didn't want to be fixed, you started the breakup process. In this, you began to remove yourself from that individual emotionally, materially and then physically. But the moment your ex noticed that you were moving out of the relationship, he or she pretended that all the work you'd done had been beneficial. For example, let's say that Morgan is dating Jeffrey (also known as Jeff). Morgan is a Christian woman with high hopes and low self-esteem. This is how Jeffrey managed to enter into her life. Jeffrey is both abusive and narcissistic, and his violent outbursts have come to be too much for Morgan to bear, so one day, she reasons within her heart that Jeff will never change. Inwardly, she rehearses in her mind that Jeff is going to be the death of her if she doesn't leave that relationship. Unbeknownst to her, by drawing this conclusion, Morgan's behavior began to shift. Her eyes did not light up anytime Jeff was in the room anymore, and she started volunteering for more hours at her job. Normally, she would turn down any chance for overtime because she wanted to spend every waking moment with Jeff. All the same, she no longer questions Jeff about his whereabouts, his late-night phone calls or his tantrums. Realizing that he's pretty much lost his girlfriend, Jeff walks up to her one Monday and says, "You know, I was talking to Brad yesterday, and I told him this—I said, man, you're gonna have to treat Dorothy better! The good Lord is not gonna stand by and let you keep hitting on His daughter. Women are precious gifts of God, and any man who doesn't value a gift that God has given him will lose that gift. Oh yeah, I tuned in to church online a few times, so I know a little something." With those words, Jeff winks at Morgan. All of a sudden, Morgan's countenance lights up. Do you understand what just happened here? Jeff, in so many ways, was Morgan's personal tower of Babel. She was building and building until she realized that her and Jeff's language had been confused, but when Jeff spoke her language, her hope was restored. By default, we value any and everything we invest time, tears, sweat and money into, and because of this, it is difficult for us to walk away from anything or any person we've invested in. Jeff knows this because Satan knows this, and Jeff is full of the devil. Jeff knew that Morgan was inwardly grieving their relationship, but he also knew that a grieving woman would do just about anything to experience relief. By speaking her language, Jeff conveyed to Morgan that she had not been building in vain. This inspired Morgan to pick up her tools and start building again.

Let's briefly discuss the protective or protector's function often found in men. This instinctive drive causes men to want to protect anything or anyone they deem to be weaker than themselves; that is, of course, if the guys in question are not broken. Whenever a toxic woman, for example, enters into a man's life or attempts to enter into his intimate space, she will often use sex to gain access to his heart, or she will tap into his protector's function. What does this look like? Imagine this—Carmen notices Phillip every time he leaves his house to head to work. Phillip is a handsome guy, but the problem is that he is a handsome MARRIED guy. Nevertheless, Carmen has a major crush on Phillip and she will stop at nothing to get what she wants. To silence the voice of the Lord in her conscious, Carmen repeatedly tells herself that Phillip's wife is a wicked woman who doesn't deserve him. She justifies this line of reasoning by constantly replaying that moment when she saw Phillip and his wife, Tamara, arguing as Phillip loaded their three-year-old daughter into his wife's car. It was clear what the argument was about. Tamara wanted Phillip to drop their daughter off at daycare, but Phillip insisted that by doing so, he would be late for work. His wife, on the other hand, wouldn't be late for work if she dropped their daughter off, even though going to the daycare would have been out of her way. On that day, Phillip stormed into the house after placing their daughter in his wife's car, and to respond to what she believed to be her husband's indignant behavior, Tamara had removed their daughter from her car seat and told her to go and knock on the door. When Phillip opened the door, his wife pulled off, but not before laughing loudly and sticking out her tongue like a two-year old. Determined to rescue Phillip from his marriage, Carmen tried to figure out a perfect excuse to initiate a conversation with Phillip, and it didn't take her long to come up with an icebreaker.

One day, Carmen walked up to Phillip as he was preparing to leave for work. His wife had already left for work, so Carmen didn't have to worry about any interference. "Excuse me!" she shouted from across the street as she approached Phillip. Phillip turned around to see an olive-complexioned woman with almond-shaped eyes, long, dark hair and the deepest dimples he'd ever seen heading his way. In other words, Carmen was breathtakingly beautiful. "Excuse me, I'm so sorry," Carmen said as she approached Phillip. "My apologies. My name is Carmen, and I live in that house right there," Carmen said pointing to her house. "I know this sounds crazy, and I promise you that

I'm not crazy, but if you ever see any strange activity taking place at my house, please call the cops. I'm just trying to let all my neighbors know about my dilemma." Phillip looks around before fixating his eyes back on Carmen. "Um, okay," he said. "Is there anything I should be looking for in particular?" Carmen smiled, revealing her beautiful white teeth and her dimples. "Yep, I look like a crazy woman. Okay, let me start over. My name is Carmen and my ex-boyfriend is trying to kill me. I broke it off with him about three months ago, and up until recently, I haven't heard from him. Yesterday, I got a call from the police department. They said that the restraining order I had protecting me from him is now expired. So, if you see any strange occurrences, like a man sitting in his car, please call 911." What Carmen is doing is trying to access Phillip's intimate circle by utilizing his protective nature. Believe it or not, this actually works! You see, Phillip will now feel responsible for guarding Carmen, especially if she submits to his instructions. He will even disregard his wife's voice if she complains about his newfound relationship with Carmen, reasoning that his wife is both insecure and insensitive. This belief will cause him to begin detaching from his wife, all the while cleaving or yoking himself to his manipulative neighbor. One day, Carmen will trick him into coming into her home, claiming that she heard a noise, and from there, she'll likely seduce him; that is, of course, after he's heroically checked and cleared the home. The lesson here is this—never allow people to manipulate their way into your intimate spaces. Stay within the will of God and always have wise counselors around you to ensure that someone with bad motives doesn't use your good intentions against you.

Your intellectual circle is like your thought life. Every thought that enters your mind must first enter into your conscious. From there, it should be tested and approved before it can enter into your heart. If bad thoughts enter into your subconscious (heart), they will begin to form or deform your reality. Your reality is predicated upon your realm (your thought domain). Bad thoughts, if not acted upon, become beliefs. Ungodly beliefs repel the truth, all the while attracting all that is ungodly. And believe it or not, your beliefs don't stabilize themselves; every thought or belief is attached to another thought or belief, but it is your core beliefs that set the stage for every other belief. So, it goes without saying that Satan passionately wants to get misinformation from your conscious to your subconscious and then into the very core of your being; this way, you will attract and be attracted to evil. In other words, you guard your heart by:

1. **Storing the truth within your soul.** David said it this way in Psalm 119:11, "Thy word have I hid in mine heart, that I might not sin against thee."

2. **Self-examination.** This is something we must do daily. We examine ourselves by comparing our thoughts, choices and results with the fruits of the Spirit.

3. **Testing the fruits; trying the spirits.** Being patient enough to examine everyone who auditions for a role in our lives and positioning each person accordingly.

4. **Getting knowledge**. Familiarizing ourselves with the many tactics and wiles of the enemy.
5. **Maturing**. How can we examine anyone else's fruits if our fruits are bitter or underdeveloped?

Relational Labels

Go into any store and you'll find that everything that's for sale has a label on it or near it. It has the name of the brand, the description of what's in the box or container (unless it's fruit or produce), the price, the bar-code and it may even advertise its benefits. But imagine this—you purchase three cans of what is advertised to be corn, and when you get home, you decide to eat the contents of one of those cans. You grab your trusted can opener and start the process of opening the can. As the metal breaks, you notice that whatever is in the can isn't yellow; it's green. You reason within yourself that maybe the lighting in your kitchen is bad, causing the corn to look green, but after the lid comes completely off the can, you are astonished. Inside the can, you find a bunch of green peas floating in water. Disgusted, you grab a fork, thinking that maybe you've just purchased an expired can of corn, but after you manage to get some of the contents out of the can, you realize that you're looking at a sea of green peas. You're upset, disappointed and hungry! The largest part of your disappointment isn't necessarily centered around the fact that you've just wasted a few bucks of your money, gas and a few moments of your time going to the store, only to be deceived into purchasing a can of peas; the greatest disappointment you feel comes from the fact that you had your heart set on eating corn that day. Of course, the customer service department at the store you purchased the peas from would be more than happy to either replace what you've purchased or give you a refund, but they wouldn't be able or willing to refund you the time you've lost or the gas you've burned. Then again, you have to decide whether or not taking the cans back to the store is even worth the effort or time, given the fact that you'll have to burn more gas and waste more time. And with this being one incident, it likely wouldn't take a great toll on your trust, but it would definitely change how you shop. Now consider this same concept in relationships.

The truth is that the majority of people are consumers; we've already established this. They are takers, and truth be told, takers don't make great friends. They can be loyal; they can be accommodating and they can be friendly, but what time teaches us all is that people are rarely loyal to people; they are loyal to the seasons that they're in. Get this—seasons aren't spaces of time, even though there is a time aspect to seasons. A season is a mindset! It is the time in which you are locked in or confined to a series of beliefs, a certain measure of information and a certain realm of revelation. When God wants to advance you forward, He simply gives you more information, along with more revelation. This information often comes through a person or a book. Once you take this information in, your worldview begins to expand. This is where Amos 3:3 comes into the picture. It reads, "Can two walk together, except they be agreed?" The people you once referred to as friends wouldn't have the revelation that you have been granted access to. Consequently, you would still be able to relate to them, but they wouldn't be able to relate to you. This is when disagreements stop popping up. Sure, they may have been extremely loyal to you in one season, but once that season ended, you would find that they are more committed to the season than they are to you. This is where disappointment enters the equation. You thought you'd found a friend in them, only to discover that once the windows of Heaven opened, your eyes opened, revealing that the people you called your friends were really enemies of your purpose.

I can revisit a few times in my life when I thought a person I was entertaining was a true friend. What I soon learned was that it is possible for you to be a friend to someone who isn't a friend of yours. I think about this one incident in particular, whereas I'd gone before God to complain about the woman who I'd allowed to call me her best friend for several years. And while she was friendly, she definitely wasn't my friend. We talked on the phone every day for hours at a time, and most of that time was spent with me listening to her talk about herself, how her day had been and what she wanted from life. I'd laugh, throw my "two cents" into the conversation and then listen for another five to ten minutes before I could jump in and say whatever I wanted to say. In truth, our conversations started looking and sounding like a good game of jump rope, whereas she'd be talking and I'd be looking for a way to jump in. Once I started talking, she'd jump in and say, "I don't mean to cut you off, but ..." After this, she'd proceed to do just that—cut me off. I don't know how I allowed this behavior for so long because I'm in no way passive. Nevertheless, after a while, we managed to normalize this behavior and it became a culture in our friendship. And again, one day, I went before the Lord in prayer about her. I complained about her being relatively narcissistic and self-centered. I don't know what I wanted the Lord to do; what I do know is that the Lord interrupted my rant with these words, "Don't tell Me; tell her." It was loud and clear. I realized at that moment that I had been fully operating in error. I was tolerating and enabling a lot of behaviors that I had trouble stomaching, in the name of friendship. So, I called her phone, but as usual, I went to voice mail. You see, over the course of time, we'd developed this unspoken rule that she'd call me. I would not call her. Again, this wasn't something we'd verbalized. It was just that I'd given up on calling her because whenever I did, she wouldn't answer her calls. I would often dismiss this behavior, reasoning within myself that she worked outside of her home, whereas I worked from home. So, I'd started letting her call me whenever she was available. I didn't realize that I was surrendering to a spirit of control; this was largely because the woman in question was passive and soft-spoken. To the naked eye, she didn't appear to be controlling; she'd never raised her voice at me, and we'd never argued. We'd always remained cordial, even when we didn't agree. But it was in that space of time that I realized that I was definitely being controlled. This is called passive control. Passive control is characterized by passive-aggressive behaviors. Mayo Clinic reports the following about passive-aggressiveness:

"Passive-aggressive behavior is a pattern of indirectly expressing negative feelings instead of openly addressing them. There's a disconnect between what a person who exhibits passive-aggressive behavior says and what he or she does. For example, someone who engages in passive-aggressive behavior might appear to agree — perhaps even enthusiastically — with another person's request. Rather than complying with the request, however, he or she might express anger or resentment by failing to follow through or missing deadlines.

Specific signs of passive-aggressive behavior include:

- Resentment and opposition to the demands of others, especially the demands of people in positions of authority.
- Resistance to cooperation, procrastination and intentional mistakes in response to others' demands.
- Cynical, sullen or hostile attitude.
- Frequent complaints about feeling underappreciated or cheated" (Source: Mayo Clinic/What is passive-aggressive behavior? What are some of the signs?/Daniel K. Hall-

Flavin, M.D.).

Again, I called my former friend, but I ended up going to her voice mail. She immediately sent me a text back saying that she'd call me back. I replied with a text letting her know that I needed to speak with her whenever she was available. Once she called me back, I shared my complaint with her and I told her that she'd never been a friend to me. This is what I had been afraid of the whole time. I was always afraid that my words would be too harsh, after all, I'd reasoned with myself that she was too fragile to handle the weight of my words. I was wrong. That day, I saw a side of her that I had never seen before. She ended up telling me (in so many words) that she had never attempted to be reciprocal because she felt like I was strong enough to handle my own issues. In other words, she didn't feel like I needed her to be a friend to me. Was she a horrible person? Absolutely not. This goes back to the corn/peas example. When I'd met her, she'd reached out to me needing counsel. I allowed what was supposed to be a mentorship-type situation to turn into something it was never intended to turn into. She wasn't a bad person. She was a babe in Christ. And get this—her behavior is common with babes! Think back to the neighbor's child who'd managed to swindle a huge bag of chips from you. That child was acting like a child! If you became best friends with the child, this would not serve as an indictment against the little boy. It would be an indictment against you! I soon realized that we were not friends. I'd simply allowed her to put the wrong label on our relationship, after all, she had been the first person to start throwing out labels. And I grew up thinking that it was rude not to reciprocate whatever kind words someone spoke. So, for example, if someone said, "I love you," I was taught to say, "I love you too." If someone said, "You are amazing," I would say, "So are you." So, when she said, "I know we haven't known each other long, but I feel like you're my best friend," I felt inclined to say, "You're my best friend as well." It took me years to unlearn this behavior. And our relationship had been decent enough; she wasn't bad or unpleasant. She was just immature. What happened here? I'd put the words "friend" and "best friend" on a can, but when I needed a friend, I went looking for one in her and couldn't find it. This is the very nature of disappointment. Nevertheless, I had been ministering to her, listening to her and being a friend to her for several years. When I reviewed our relationship, it became evident that I was her mentor! Why is this important? Had I known this from the beginning, I would not have:

1. Given up so much of my time.
2. Given up my time so freely.
3. Availed myself to her so frequently.
4. Shared intimate details about my life.
5. Leaned on her whenever I found myself in need of a friend.

All the same, that friendship would not have ended the way it had. That was the friendship that made me reevaluate myself and the people I had around me. This made me realize that I had a savior complex. Healthline reports the following:

> "A savior complex, or white knight syndrome, describes this need to "save" people by fixing their problems.
> If you have a savior complex, you might:

> - only feel good about yourself when helping someone.
> - believe helping others is your purpose.
> - expend so much energy trying to fix others that you end up burning out.

> Here's a look at how to recognize this kind of behavior and why it can do more harm than good" (Source: Healthline/Always Trying to 'Save' People? You Might Have a Savior Complex).

You see, labels aren't just for the people around us; we have to diagnose our own issues as well. The moment I'd gone to God about her, I was in a burnout phase. I couldn't imagine talking to her or tolerating her another day. But again, the issue wasn't that she was a bad person; the problem was a simple misplacement of labels. This is something we have all been guilty of. We'd placed the wrong labels on our relationships, only for those relationships to end in offense. I was always the "strong friend" in relationships; this would always end in me feeling used, depleted, unappreciated and frustrated. I had to learn that there is no such thing as the strong friend. Read that again. If you are always the proverbial strong friend, the people who you're entertaining are not your friends. Chances are, they are:

1. Your mentees.
2. Your baby sisters or brothers in Christ.
3. Opportunists.
4. People whose friendship you've purchased.

There is absolutely nothing wrong with anyone being a mentee or a babe in Christ. What I learned over the years is that people who are immature in the faith can be impatient and overly determined to build friendships with other people. This is especially true in the consumer/producer dynamic. Consumers see producers as invaluable, so whenever they come in contact with a producer or a problem-solver, they try to rush the relationship. I've hosted many classes and mentorship programs, and I find this behavior to be, not only common, but absolutely annoying. All too often, people register for one of my programs, and they'll repeatedly try to go around the systems and the people I have in place to regulate those programs. When we point out the boundaries and guidelines to them, they immediately get offended and start feeling rejected. So, I have spent quite a bit of time trying to teach them relational acuity, helping them to understand that their need to be seen, acknowledged, stand out from the crowd and favored stems from, in many cases, the fear of rejection and the fear of abandonment. You see, people sometimes think that if they don't hurry up and build value in a relationship, they will be abandoned or overlooked. This is because they were likely born into toxic environments and they've been surrounded by toxic people their entire lives. Of course, this causes them to become toxic, but get this—people with good intentions don't realize that they are toxic because their judgment is clouded by their good intentions. Nevertheless, their dysfunctional ways show up whenever they come face-to-face with a set of boundaries. This is because bound people hate boundaries. And while they may be good people with a relatively stable moral compass, the truth is, they don't understand relational acuity because no one has ever taught them about the different types of relationships that they'll have over the courses of their lives. Consequently, they view everyone as their friends, and they deal with the perpetual sting of disappointment every time someone in their lives proves to be an opportunist.

So, what are the proper labels?
1. Friend
2. Close Friend
3. Best Friend
4. Sister or Brother in Christ
5. Associate
6. Confidante
7. Mentor/Teacher
8. Mentee/Protege
9. Client

Friend: People who fit into this category have proven themselves to be trustworthy, loyal, intentional and selfless. But again, remember that this doesn't mean that they are your personal friend; they can be loyal to the season that you're in, making them a seasonal connection. Nevertheless, they are purposeful and they may even be God-established fixtures in your life for the seasons you're in. Jonathan was a friend of David, but he was a seasonal fixture. You may find yourself speaking with a friend every few days to every few years.

Close Friend: This is someone who has a purpose in your life; someone you've come to trust with some of the most intimate details of your life. When times are tough, this is the person you'll likely think about. You may find yourself speaking with a close friend every few days to every few months.

Best Friend: In my experience, this can be a relatively dangerous label to place on someone if you don't understand the concept of a season. We tend to call people our "best friends" when we are in our twenties and early thirties, but you'll find that a lot of older men and women don't use these labels so frequently. Do best friends exist? Yes, they do, but they are extremely rare in function, but not so much in title. What this means is that the label "best friends" is passed around freely and frequently, but the function is oftentimes one-sided. Again, consider the consumer/producer dynamic. In many of these relationships, you will find a consumer and you will find a producer with a savior's complex. They've developed a dependency or a codependent relationship, whereas they manage to satisfy one another's insecurities by forming an alliance that is centered around their own personal needs. In other words, they are both (in many cases) self-centered. Howbeit, in a real best-friendship, you will find people who are not only trusting of one another with their time and properties, they trust each other with their lives. This is the friend that sticks closer than a brother (or sister). You may find yourself speaking with a best friend every day or every few days.

Sister or Brother in Christ: This particular label can be broken down into categories:

1. A little sister/brother in Christ: this is someone who is more needy or more of a consumer in the relationship.
2. A sister/brother in Christ: this is a balanced relationship, whereas both parties are reciprocal of one another's good deeds, love and time, thus rendering the relationship mutually beneficial.
3. A big sister/brother in Christ: this is someone who is more of a mentor/producer in the relationship.

Amazingly enough, I've discovered that you can find sisters and brothers in Christ who are closer and more loyal to you than your closest friends. This is because these relationships can be and sometimes are centered around purpose and not persons. Some of these relationships are God-established, and what makes them so powerful is that you can go months and years without speaking with one another and still be as close as you were when you last spoke. There is no competition, no demand and no offense; there is simply the freedom to be who you are without the fear of rejection or abandonment plaguing the relationship should you not give into a bunch of unspoken rules.

Associate: This is a person who you simply affiliate yourself with. You are kind to one another and you may even encourage and help one another. Nevertheless, you will find in these relationships that there is no need for labels and no demand or expectation. These are typically some of the people you work with or go to church with. We call them workplace buddies or church friends. You may find yourself going out to eat with them and even sharing a detail or two about your life, but what keeps these relationships from being labeled as friendships is the fact that there is no true or consistent pursuit outside of the workplace, church or wherever you commonly see one another.

Confidante: The word "confidant" is defined by Oxford Languages this way: "a person with whom one shares a secret or private matter, trusting them not to repeat it to others." A confidante may be someone you aren't necessarily friends with, but you've come to trust. These are the people you may find yourself leaning on in hard times, especially when you don't know anywhere else to turn or when the people you normally confide in are too immature or too inexperienced to be trusted with whatever burdens you are carrying. They may be the burdens that you are needing help with. A confidante could be that older janitor at your job or that quiet young woman at your church who appears to be wise beyond her years. We stumble upon these people when we are in the midst of our storms. For example, I can remember breaking down in a former manager's office and confiding in her about what I had been experiencing in my life. This wasn't planned. I simply wanted to go home because I felt that I was too fragile and emotionally compromised to perform. I went to her office to ask to go home, and before I could finish my sentence, I began to weep uncontrollably. I was ashamed, of course, because I don't like to cry in front of people, but I needed the counsel that she gave me thereafter. After this, she would ask me how I was doing and if I needed anything. She wasn't my friend and she didn't become my mentor. She was simply someone I confided in when I didn't know where else to turn.

Mentor/Teacher: This is a beautiful role to hold, but it can be one of the most frustrating labels because a large number of people in the western world do not understand the concept of rank, authority and leadership. Because of this, they try to fit everyone into the same box which, of course, is the friend zone. The problem with this behavior is when you refer to your mentor as your friend, the relationship will become imbalanced. You will expect more from the mentor, all the while giving him or her your bare minimum. Again, this leads to hurt feelings, offense, disappointment and broken relationships. This can also lead to you feeling entitled to the mentor's time and resources. Remember that the mentor is someone who pours into you. This is someone who may exceed or excel in a role that you want to excel in. They are not confidantes, even though you can confide in them. It is not uncommon for people to confuse their mentors with their confidantes and their confidantes with their mentors. The difference between the two is:

1. The confidante is someone you confide in about an issue, oftentimes in the heat of a moment. You will only speak with the confidante about that particular issue whenever you bump into him or her.
2. The mentor is someone you intentionally seek to learn about something in particular. Again, the mentor may be strong in an area that you are weak or knowledgeable in an area that you want to grow in. Mentorships are rarely, if ever, centered around emotions or emotional situations. Mentorship is about your future and not so much your past.

Mentee: A mentee can become a menace if he or she does not immediately come in contact with rules and boundaries. Again, this is because a lot of people were never taught about the different types of relationships they can have. I immediately think about a woman who registered for my mentorship program who didn't last two weeks in the program. She wasn't the first and only woman to have such a short tenure in the program, but she was definitely the most memorable because of how easily offended she was. I remember that after she'd attended the first class Zoom call, she'd emailed me. Now, before this particular incident, she'd already emailed me several times complaining about not knowing how to navigate her way around the classroom. I knew then that she wouldn't last long. And when she attended the first class, all seemed well until after the call. She emailed me to accuse some of the students of making fun of her. Not one student had made fun of her or referenced her in any way. Her incredibly long email was filled with emotionalism. I assured her that none of the students had been making indirect references to her in the chat; they were simply communicating with one another. A week later, she emailed me again, accusing the students of making fun of her again. In that email, she confirmed what I already suspected. She wasn't mentally and emotionally healthy; I was more than sure that she was schizophrenic based on a lot of what she'd said in her email. I kept thinking to myself that I needed to refund her and send her on her way because she was genuinely paranoid about everything. One day, she emailed me and said, "Please send me your number so I can call you." I emailed her back, letting her know that none of the students had my personal number, and if she needed to set up a call with me, she had to fill out the form to start the process. Her response was emotional; she questioned why she was in the program if she couldn't call me at will. I had over one hundred women in my mentorship program; there was no way I was about to give out my phone number to one hundred people to call me whenever they wanted to, otherwise, I wouldn't be able to function in any other role. There has to be order in all things. Of course, she sent me back an emotional email demanding a refund, and I happily gave it to her because I hadn't been able to shake the thought that I needed to refund her and refer her to someone who could better assist her. Without the proper boundaries, this woman would have become a menace in my life and to the other ladies I was mentoring. She would have tried to create a bunch of ungodly soul ties, and she would have brought chaos to the program by constantly accusing the women of talking about her or plotting against her. A mentee, of course, is the student of a mentor. They submit to a schedule and/or a program to learn a specific trade, sharpen a specific gift or grow in a specific area. The goal of the mentee is to become like the mentor or to reach the mentor's level in an area. After this, the mentee can either function at that level or find someone greater than his or her mentor to help the mentee to excel in that particular area.

Acquaintance: An acquaintance is someone who exchanges something to acquire something in return. This isn't always something that takes place in the marketplace. For example, I may say to someone at my church, "How do you apply your eyelashes? I've always wanted to know." The person may reply, for example, "What are you doing on Friday? You can come by my house, and I'll show you." While this person is my sister in Christ, she wouldn't be my mentor; we would be acquaintances. This means that the only reason I'd be going to her house would be to learn how to apply eyelashes. Of course, we could develop a closer relationship over time, but at that moment, the best label to assume is that I would be her acquaintance.

Of course, there are many other labels that we can assume, but these are the most important ones. Placing the proper labels on your relationships will ensure:
1. That they last longer.
2. There is little to no room for offense.
3. That they are extremely beneficial.
4. That you don't burn one another out.
5. That neither of you is taken advantage of.

6. That no one is traumatized in the long haul.
7. The two of you walk in agreement, which ensures that your relationship is healthy, and where there is good health, you will find the healing properties of love, respect, honor and understanding.
8. You can readily distinguish the consumers from the producers and move accordingly.

RELATIONAL PROTOCOL

With every label, there is protocol. For example, Rebekah befriends Veronica, and while there is nothing wrong with two people becoming friends, the problem is that Rebekah is relatively immature and needy. Veronica, on the other hand, is independent, self-sufficient, strong and responsible. Their relationship will undoubtedly be one-sided if Veronica does not do her due diligence by testing the spirit, as the Bible tells us to, and by setting the necessary boundaries to ensure that Rebekah doesn't take advantage of her. To do this, of course, she'd have to place the right label on the relationship, and this takes time. Again, there is nothing wrong with being a consumer, but consumers consume while producers produce. And understand this—it would be hard for Rebekah to respect a position she's never held. What I mean is—Rebekah may not respect time because she often wastes her time, rather than using it wisely. Because of this, she won't respect Veronica's time. So, she may want to spend a considerable amount of time talking over the phone about minor things, and this could cost Veronica a great deal of money and cause her to lose her productive pace. Think about it this way—Veronica makes bundt cakes for a living, but her roommate, Rebekah, consumes those cakes at the rate in which she makes them. Rebekah would run Veronica out of business if the proper boundaries were not put in place; we understand this, but what if Veronica allowed Rebekah to define their relationship? After all, the people who benefit the most in a relationship are oftentimes the ones who attempt to define and label it. This is to ensure that they can extract the most benefits from that relationship. What if Rebekah called herself Veronica's business partner? Do you see how detrimental this would be? The same concept applies to friendships and other relationship types. Going back to the first example, if Veronica doesn't immediately recognize that she has more to lose than Rebekah, she will find herself being taken advantage of. This doesn't mean that Rebekah is a bad person. It simply means that Rebekah is a consumer, and consumers are driven by demand. In short, there are two laws in operation here. They are supply and demand. And while these laws are used in the marketplace, they can also be used in the realm of relationships. Check out the following article.

> "The law of supply and demand is a theory that explains the interaction between the sellers of a resource and the buyers for that resource. The theory defines the relationship between the price of a given good or product and the willingness of people to either buy or sell it. Generally, as price increases, people are willing to supply more and demand less and vice versa when the price falls" (Source: Investopedia/ Law of Supply and Demand/ Jason Fernando).

Investopedia also reports the following:
- "The law of supply is the microeconomic law that states that, all other factors being equal, as the price of a good or service increases, the quantity of

goods or services that suppliers offer will increase, and vice versa. The law of supply says that as the price of an item goes up, suppliers will attempt to maximize their profits by increasing the number of items for sale" (Source: Investopedia/ Law of Supply/ Investopedia Team).

- "The law of demand states that the quantity purchased varies inversely with price. In other words, the higher the price, the lower the quantity demanded. This occurs because of diminishing marginal utility. That is, consumers use the first units of an economic good they purchase to serve their most urgent needs first, and then they use each additional unit of the good to serve successively lower-valued ends" (Source: Investopedia/ Law of Demand/ Adam Hayes).

In this case, Veronica would be the seller/solutionist/producer, whereas Rebekah would be the buyer/user/consumer. Let's say that the demand was money. Rebekah has been struggling with her finances for as far back as she can remember. Veronica, on the other hand, has a bundt cake company and she's doing well financially. The two women meet at a conference and they hit it off. They exchange numbers and plan to hang out in the near future. They're both decent and moral women; there is absolutely nothing wrong with them connecting. As a matter of fact, it is possible that God connected the women. But again, the right label would have to be placed on this relationship to ensure both women extract all of the benefits from it; this way, they can be beneficial to one another. Rebekah is driven by the law of demand, so she spends a great deal of time talking about what she doesn't have and what she's going through. Veronica spends a great deal of time talking about the success of her company. This infuriates Rebekah because she believes that Veronica is rubbing her success in her face, but this isn't true. Veronica is having the same conversation with Rebekah as she has with her other friends, but it goes without saying that her other friends are relatively successful, so to them, it doesn't sound like Veronica is boasting. They all typically talk about their successes and their failures, and Veronica happens to be in a season of success. At the same time, Rebekah's whining is emotionally taxing and draining to Veronica. Do you see why the proper label would be needed here? If they called their relationship a friendship, chances are, they would both remain offended with one another. This is what happens when we place the wrong labels on relationships. And get this—we are multidimensional creatures, meaning there are many sides to us. In other words, it is possible for them to be friends in one area while completely at odds in another area. For example, in the financial arena, Veronica would serve more as a mentor; that is, if Rebekah is willing to serve as a mentee. But they may be on the same page as it relates to one of their hobbies. Let's say that both women absolutely love to paint, and they are both really good at it. Their passion for painting would allow them to connect as friends in this particular area, but it would be best practice for Veronica to link herself to Rebekah financially, other than serving as a mentor. Why is this? Again, Rebekah is driven by demand in this area, whereas Veronica is driven by the law of supply. If the ladies link up the wrong way, Rebekah will reason within her own mind that Veronica should help her whenever she needs help. This will create a codependent relationship, and the only person who will benefit from this relationship will be Rebekah. Veronica, on the other hand, will begin to feel used and taken advantage of. Again, this sets the stage for offense, and this relationship would end badly, but not because either of the women is bad. Instead, they'd fight their way to freedom because entitlement would enter the picture, causing Rebekah to repeatedly beg and borrow from Veronica. This is why you will rarely if ever, see a rich man be best friends with a poor man. This may sound offensive, but it has nothing to do with the rich man "thinking he's better" than the poor guy. It has everything to do with the fact that the rich man could potentially endanger himself if he linked up to the poor guy in the wrong way. Again, this isn't to say that they cannot and should not link up; it is to say that when the law of supply and the law of demand come in close proximity with one another, there has to be rules, boundaries and allowances. Another example is—many companies won't hire people whose credit scores are low, especially if those people are applying for jobs that would allow them access to money. This is because America is a capitalistic nation, and because our country is driven by capitalism, our greatest crimes are centered around money. A great deal of these crimes were nonviolent crimes committed in the workplace, so employers soon learned that needy people can't be trusted in certain areas and departments. They could be great employees in some areas, but it is not good to place them around the very thing that they need the most. Again, this same rule applies in relationships like that of Veronica and Rebekah. I immediately think back to a couple I'd once ministered to. Because they felt like I had more to give, they took far more than they gave. This isn't to say that relationships should be centered around what we can give or what we can receive; this is to say that whenever a person has a need, that person will oftentimes gravitate towards and be attracted to people who can potentially fill that need because that individual is driven by the law of demand. In other words, the individual in question is in what I call "survival mode."

What is "survival mode"? Think about it this way. A young woman is a single mother to three young boys. The fathers of her children have all abandoned her and their sons. This created relational/romantic trauma. Again, we are multidimensional people. Every part of who we are is linked to another dimension of our being. Think of every facet of you as a state. There is a daughter state; this is where you first get your understanding of authority and love. This state directly neighbors your spousal/romantic state. Both of these states are wrapped around your financial state, and of course, these are states of mind. Because the young lady in question has been traumatized in the parental state and in the romantic state, chances are, her financial state will be in ruins. This will cause her to go into survival mode, meaning she will try to repair the ruins of one state by compromising in another. So, she may meet a man who is twenty years her senior, and even though she's not attracted to him, she may find herself entertaining a romantic relationship with him because he could and would potentially serve as a father figure, a lover and a provider. Let's say that the older guy is insecure, abusive and unstable. Because the woman lives in survival mode, she would likely endure the abuse, reasoning within herself that she's at fault for his anger, that she needs him to provide for her and her sons and the relationship would get better once she learned to avoid his triggers. A more mild example would be a man who lived at home with his mother. Because he has never learned to endure the pressures that come with having a job, the man is relatively lazy and he lacks ambition. Consequently, he spends every day of his life at home playing video games. His mother threatens him time and time again, demanding that he get a job. One day, his mother says to him that she's giving him thirty days to find a job, and after that, she's going to evict him from her home. This guy is in survival mode. Survival mode, also known as survivor's mode, is not always activated by a need to survive. It can be activated by a single demand. He needs a place to stay, but he's not willing to get a job because he hates the pressures associated with waking up and going to work. So, the son meets a few young ladies, but he puts a great deal of his attention on Erica. Let's say that his name is Bill. Erica is not the prettiest or the smartest woman in the lineup of women that he's seducing, but she is the most financially stable woman. After all, she's an accountant who owns her own home. At the same time, Erica's self-esteem is not healthy, so Bill begins to pursue her all the more. This is because Bill wants to move in with Erica, but he doesn't want to help her with the bills. Bill is in survival mode; this state of mind causes people to become manipulative. It also causes them to objectify other people as they focus on getting their needs met. Believe it or not, a great deal of consumers are in survival mode, but get this—when two consumers link up as friends, they can be relatively good to one another, but remember, they aren't necessarily loyal to the other person. They are loyal to the seasons they're in and they are loyal to their needs. This is why they can remain friends for the rest of their lives if neither of the parties graduates from that particular season.

Any time we begin to establish a relationship with other people, we must first pay attention to what they say, what roles they are attempting to assume in our lives, the roles they want us to assume in their lives, and what they are offering in exchange for what they are requiring, their histories with others, and more importantly, their relationships with God. Traditionally, we've established most of our relationships based on our voids. Voids are empty spaces in our lives. Consequently, narcissistic people have managed to find roles that they could assume in our lives in exchange for our time, our resources and our peace. Make no mistake about it—everything we do is in exchange for something else. There is no such thing as "free" except, of course, for the freedom availed to us through Jesus Christ. For example, whenever a person walks up to you, that person wants something, whether it's your attention, your time, your friendship and the list goes on. The objective is to think like an entrepreneur by assessing what they want versus what they're offering.

This sounds transactional, but it isn't. As an entrepreneur, I don't barter with people, nor do I allow them to talk me down on my prices. For example, I own a seal and logo design company, and one of my most popular packages allows my clients to get one free revision on their designs, should they need one. Additional revisions are priced at $49. It is not uncommon for me to have a client who utilizes their free revision, only to realize that he or she wants to make another change. Well, the second revision isn't free. Whenever I'm dealing with a manipulative client, that client will attempt to go around protocol by calling me, rather than filling out the revision form and paying for the upgrade. The client will then try to devalue and undermine the process by saying something like, "I just need one small or minor change." Of course, I refer the customer back to the form and remind them that the fee for this particular revision is $49. This is not welcomed news, of course, and the client already knew this. "I just need you to add the establishment date," the client objects. I allow the client to finish speaking before chiming in. "I understand, but you've already utilized your free revision, and as you can see on our website, every additional revision is $49." The client is unmoved in most cases. "I understand, but I only need one small change!" I then have to help the client to understand that all revisions are $49 each, regardless of how small they may appear to be, and I express to the client that using the word "small" does not lessen the amount of work that we have to do. So again, whenever someone walks up to you, you have to find out what they want, so you can determine if what they're giving is as valuable as what they're seeking. Going back to the Veronica/Rebekah example. Rebekah is the consumer; Veronica is the producer. Rebekah represents demand, whereas Veronica represents supply. If all Rebekah has to offer is her time and a friendship label, but in exchange, she expects Veronica to give her the time she would normally give to her bundt cake company, and she expects Veronica to help her out financially, this isn't an even exchange. Instead, Rebekah would drain Veronica of her time and resources, and then discard her once she has nothing else to offer or once she puts a solid set of boundaries in place. This would mean that the ladies could not be financial friends, even though they may be hobby friends since they both love to paint. If I were Veronica, I would avoid any talks about money with Rebekah; that is, unless I'm mentoring her. I would try to avoid loaning her any money. Instead, I'd try to help her to acquire a new skill or find a better job. This is the greatest test of motives because people who want to leech off other people often become offended when the people they're targeting start offering them solutions and not supplies.

Relational protocol has everything to do with the proper placement of people in relationships. It is centered around identifying solutionists/producers vs. takers/consumers. It also boils down to understanding rank and where each party stands in every state of their beings. Every role and rank has its own unique set of boundaries; these boundaries are designed to quarantine the survivor aspect of an individual, all the while encouraging the producer within that individual to come forth. In other words, you can never truly help someone whenever your relationship with that person is centered around pacifying them.

Relational Poverty

Poverty, contrary to popular belief, is not the absence of money. It is the absence of wisdom. The lack of money is just a byproduct of a lack of wisdom. Now, this isn't to say that everyone who lives in poverty or underneath the poverty line isn't wise. After all, you will find wise people in just about every sector of life. However, if you find a wise man or woman living in poverty, just know one or more of these factors are true:

1. They are not broke. They're either hiding money in their homes (underneath mattresses, in books, in attics, etc.), or they have plenty of money in their bank accounts. They have chosen, for one reason or another, to live simple lives.

2. While they are wise, they are both fearful and comfortable, meaning they have not and will not use their wisdom to acquire wealth. In many cases, people like this tend to be extremely family-oriented and they are afraid of what money would do to their families.

3. While they are relatively broke, they know how to acquire money or resources anytime they need them. Again, it is highly likely that they fear wealth and all that comes with it.

4. They give every dime of what they acquire to family members and/or strangers who are in need of help.

5. They are saving up their money for something.

Simply put, wisdom attracts wealth, and wealth often causes people to become even more attracted to wisdom. Consequently, they go out and acquire more wisdom which, in turn, causes more wealth to be attracted to them. This is the cycle of prosperity, and those who get caught up in this whirlpool rarely come out of it. Consider a portion of Solomon's story. 1 Kings 3:4-13 reads, "And the king went to Gibeon to sacrifice there; for that was the great high place: a thousand burnt offerings did Solomon offer upon that altar. In Gibeon the LORD appeared to Solomon in a dream by night: and God said, Ask what I shall give thee. And Solomon said, Thou hast shewed unto thy servant David my father great mercy, according as he walked before thee in truth, and in righteousness, and in uprightness of heart with thee; and thou hast kept for him this great kindness, that thou hast given him a son to sit on his throne, as it is this day. And now, O LORD my God, thou hast made thy servant king instead of David my father: and I am but a little child: I know not how to go out or come in. And thy servant is in the midst of thy people which thou hast chosen, a great people, that cannot be numbered nor counted for multitude. Give therefore thy servant an understanding heart to judge thy people, that I may discern between good and bad: for who is able to judge this thy so great a people? And the speech pleased the Lord, that Solomon had asked this thing. And God said unto him, Because thou hast asked this thing, and hast not asked for thyself long life; neither hast asked riches for thyself, nor hast asked the life of thine enemies; but hast asked for thyself understanding to discern judgment; Behold, I have done according to thy words: lo, I have given thee a wise and an understanding heart; so that there was none like thee before thee, neither after thee shall any arise like unto thee. And I have also given thee that which thou hast not asked, both riches, and honor: so that there shall not be any among the kings like unto thee all thy days." Notice in the aforementioned story that of all the things Solomon could have asked for, in his selflessness, he asked for wisdom. This prayer pleased the Lord, and He not only granted Solomon wisdom, but He gave him wealth and honor as well. Why is this significant? Because it gives us insight into the heart and the mind of God. Wealth is attracted to wisdom, and so is honor. Honor is important because it teaches people to respond to rank and act accordingly. It is a curse to be surrounded by dishonorable people, but if you are surrounded by people who understand and respond properly to rank, protocol and order, you have been favored by God. The blessings of God will always precede, encompass and follow order.

Walmart was the first job I'd ever had. I started working there when I was just 17-years old, and I worked there for seven years. When I was 18, I started working on the floor, starting with the ladies' department, and then I moved to the lingerie department. I mainly answered the phone, but I also helped in the department. One of the events I remember the most was the beginning of every month. During that space of history, most people who were on public assistance would get their checks on the first of the month. And because of this, the store would be jam-packed every month on the first. We would have to work overtime, typically from the first to about the third, because the store would be crowded and the shoppers would pretty much destroy the store. Nevertheless, by the end of the week, most people would be either broke or nearly broke again, and the store would return to its normal operations. Having grown up on public assistance, I understood (but didn't agree with) the mindset behind this behavior. You see, what the spirit of poverty does is it robs people of their authority; it pretty much limits where they can live, and it gives them an allowance of their own money. So, for the majority of the month, a lot of the people felt helpless, hopeless and hungry. But then, the first of the month would come, and all of a sudden, the people's hope seemed to be restored; they felt in control again. I'm not in any way saying that everyone who is on public assistance is a victim because many are not. I am saying that when poverty is all you know, you will think, reason and behave like a victim. That is, of course, until someone points out to you that you have the power to break free. It goes without saying that most people who were raised in poverty lack financial intelligence, so they spend almost all of the money that they have on the first day because of the adrenaline they experience while shopping. This adrenaline comes as a result of the mental warfare that they've experienced every day leading up to the first. You see, Satan overwhelms a person's mind with thoughts of what he or she doesn't have, should have and could have. He also whispers, "You only live once. Buy the lobster, buy the steak; as a matter of fact, get three packs!" He then takes the person's peace away by overwhelming the individual with thoughts of shopping and eating out. You see, when a person lives in poverty, that individual is accustomed to only having a certain amount of money in his or her account. For example, let's create a character named Betty. Betty works at a popular retail store, but the money she earns is not enough to provide for her and her three children. So, Betty turns to the system for help. For more than 12 years, Betty has always managed to maintain around one hundred bucks after paying all of her bills, and while she has typically spent this by the first of the month, it's a standard number for her.

One day, Betty receives a check in the mail for $2,239.64. As it turns out, the IRS has garnished the father of Betty's eldest two children, so the check she received was back-pay. Elated, Betty rushes to the mall and buys a few outfits for her children. All the same, she buys herself two dresses, four pairs of pants and three pairs of shoes. She then goes to get her lashes done at a station that has been set up in the middle of the mall, and she makes a hair appointment with her favorite stylist. By the time Betty returns home, she's spent $1,476.52, leaving her with $762.12. "I got the children a few outfits and uniforms for school, so I'm good now," she reasons with herself. "I can't spend any more money." Nevertheless, the next day, Betty realizes that their refrigerator is nearly empty. It Is the 23rd of the month, and her check from public assistance wouldn't arrive until the first. While they were normally able to make due with what they had, at this point, they don't have to scrap for food because Betty has well over $700 in her account. So, she goes to the supermarket and spends $376.88, leaving her with $386.24. "I've got to stop spending!" Betty shouts as she unloads the bags from her car. Howbeit, later that night, Betty orders pizza for her and her family, she gives each child $20 each, and the next day, she spends over $100 at a water park. Two days later, Betty has $118.76 left in her account. "Let's go out to eat," she says to one of her coworkers just before she clocks out for her lunch break. What happened to Betty is common. Because she's accustomed to only seeing $100 or less in her bank account, anytime there is an overage of that amount, she loses her peace. She can't stop thinking about what she wants, what she needs and what everyone else has. Her peace doesn't return until she has $100 or less in her account. This is just how poverty works. It causes people to become hyper-aware of the fact that they have more money in their accounts than they are accustomed to. Thoughts of clothes, shoes and food will invade and overwhelm the person's mind until the individual spends the majority of the money in his or her account. Please note that warfare can oftentimes feel good to the soul, but its aftertaste is bitter. I shared how financial poverty works so that you could understand how relational poverty works.

Relational poverty is not the absence of relationships, it is the absence of qualitative relationships. It means to be surrounded by unwise, foolish or dishonorable people. Believe it or not, this (within itself) is a siege of sorts. What is a siege? Oxford Languages defines it this way, "a military operation in which enemy forces surround a town or building, cutting off essential supplies, with the aim of compelling the surrender of those inside." The goal of a siege is to cut off access to the outside world, thus causing a kingdom to suffer through famines and droughts. Hungry, thirsty and terrified, the people begin to compromise their values, their beliefs and their lifestyles to survive. In relational poverty, the enemy seeks to create a drought of God's Word by causing people to surround themselves with what the Bible refers to as "bad company." Additionally, where there is no water (Word), there will be no bread (deliverance) because you can't make bread without water. In other words, you can't cast out demons without the Word. This creates a siege-like effect, where the people don't necessarily have anywhere to turn to look for wisdom, knowledge or to acquire understanding. Instead, the people feed on foolishness (gossip, slander, complaints, misinformation). And remember, one of the blessings that God bestowed upon Solomon after he'd asked for wisdom was honor! In relational poverty, there is no understanding of honor. As a matter of fact, if you want to offend someone in relational poverty, mention the words "honor" and "submission." This is why narcissists thrive so much in these communities. It allows them to usurp the authority of others and exalt themselves as ringmasters and authority figures over a bunch of small to medium-sized groups. In relational poverty, almost everyone is a consumer; there are few producers. And whenever a producer begins to develop around consumers, that producer is often taken advantage of, traumatized and abused.

Relational poverty is almost always the result of dishonor,

either by the individual or someone in that person's generational lineage. Consider this—Lucifer got kicked out of Heaven because he tried to make himself equal with God. In Isaiah 14:12-14, the Lord rebukes Lucifer with these words, "How art thou fallen from heaven, O Lucifer, son of the morning! How art thou cut down to the ground, which didst weaken the nations! For thou hast said in thine heart, I will ascend into heaven, I will exalt my throne above the stars of God: I will sit also upon the mount of the congregation, in the sides of the north: I will ascend above the heights of the clouds; I will be like the most High." Romans 13:1-7 states, "Let every soul be subject unto the higher powers. For there is no power but of God: the powers that be are ordained of God. Whosoever therefore resisteth the power, resisteth the ordinance of God: and they that resist shall receive to themselves damnation. For rulers are not a terror to good works, but to the evil. Wilt thou then not be afraid of the power? Do that which is good, and thou shalt have praise of the same: For he is the minister of God to thee for good. But if thou do that which is evil, be afraid; for he beareth not the sword in vain: for he is the minister of God, a revenger to execute wrath upon him that doeth evil. Wherefore ye must needs be subject, not only for wrath but also for conscience sake. For for this cause pay ye tribute also: for they are God's ministers, attending continually upon this very thing. Render therefore to all their dues: tribute to whom tribute is due; custom to whom custom; fear to whom fear; honor to whom honor." Protocol is a part of God's system, and whenever people rise against order and protocol, they are also rejecting God's system. God is

Light, meaning that in Him, there is no darkness; there is instead glory and revelation. Without revelation, what's left is darkness. Where is darkness found again? In voids! What this means is that whenever we reject and come against the ordinances of God, we set the stage for:

1. **Rejection:** We cause God to reject us and whatever it is that we're building (consider the Tower of Babel) because we chose to reject Him by rejecting His ordinances.

2. **Dishonor:** Dishonor is a disability within itself. It is the inability to recognize or respect authority figures. It is the very core of entitlement. And wherever there is dishonor, there will be strife. Where there is strife, there will be every evil work (see James 3:16). Where there is every evil work, there will be evil workers (demons).

3. **Rebellion:** When dishonor enters the picture, people begin to come against those who were set in place to lead movements, ministries and the like. This causes the people to compete with one another for power, which then sets the stage for splits, wars and massacres. This is the very nature of rebellion, and according to 1 Samuel 15:23, rebellion is like the sin of witchcraft.

4. **Witchcraft:** Any power that is absent of God is witchcraft, and when witchcraft enters the picture, so does Satan and his workers.

5. **Financial Poverty:** Wealth follows wisdom, and wisdom is the heart and mind of God, so when God exits a system, a family or a community, financial prosperity follows suit.

Let's create two characters. We'll call them Billy and Bob. Billy has 23 friends, with five of them being in Circle 1, eight of them being in Circle 2, seven of them being in Circle 3 and three of them being in Circle 4. None of Billy's friends are his mentors; instead, the men completely disregard the concept of rank and protocol. Note that every friendship group has someone who unofficially serves as the leader of that group, and in Billy's circle, Jonathan has taken on this role. The problem with this is the fact that while Jonathan is loud, aggressive and somewhat bold, he is also a foolish man. Bob, on the other hand, has two friends. One of them is in Circle 1 and the other is in Circle 4. The friend in Circle 1 serves as Bob's mentor most of the time, but the two are friends as well. The guy in Circle 4, while friends with Bob, sees Bob as his mentor. Which of the two guys do you believe is richer? To the naked eye, most people would proclaim that Billy is richer. After all, you'd likely see a lot of posts popping up on social media from Billy displaying all of the fun adventures that he and his friends have embarked upon. And if relational prosperity was determined by fun, Billy would take home the win. Bob, of course, is richer because there is structure to his relationships, so you won't see as much strife, confusion or competition as you'd see in some of Billy's dealings. Bob's relationships will likely last a lifetime, whereas Billy's relationships will all fizzle out over time. Billy's friends may be a siege wall around his soul, keeping him from advancing in life and in the Kingdom of God. This isn't to say that if you have a lot of friends, you are doomed. It is to say that you should examine all of your relationships to ensure that everyone is in their proper circle.

Relational prosperity doesn't necessarily mean that you will only have a handful of friends. Consider this truth—a woman who dies to herself and meets another woman who has died to herself in Christ is a blessed woman. If she meets another woman who is fully surrendered to the Most High God, she has tangible favor. If she meets and bonds with another woman or man after God's own heart, she is blessed and highly favored! In the Kingdom of God, our relationships are currency, but not all relationships are equal in value. And relational prosperity doesn't always involve us finding people who are sold out for Christ; it's also teaching people to fully surrender themselves to Christ. In other words, when we are able to surrender wholeheartedly to the Lord and then teach others to do the same, we become like a tree planted by the rivers. We then reproduce the fruits that are thriving in our lives.

FAMILIARITY AND DISHONOR

Consider the plight of Moses' sister, Miriam. She'd played
a major role in her brother's life, starting with the moment
she watched her mother load Moses into a basket and then
place the basket in the sea. Miriam stood afar off,
watching her brother float until Pharaoh's daughter found
him. Let's look at the story. Exodus 2:1-10 reads, "And
there went a man of the house of Levi, and took to wife a
daughter of Levi. And the woman conceived, and bare a
son: and when she saw him that he was a goodly child, she
hid him three months. And when she could not longer hide
him, she took for him an ark of bulrushes, and daubed it
with slime and with pitch, and put the child therein; and
she laid it in the flags by the river's brink. And his sister
stood afar off, to wit what would be done to him.
And the daughter of Pharaoh came down to wash herself
at the river; and her maidens walked along by the river's
side; and when she saw the ark among the flags, she sent
her maid to fetch it. And when she had opened it, she saw
the child: and, behold, the babe wept. And she had
compassion on him, and said, This is one of the Hebrews'
children. Then said his sister to Pharaoh's daughter, Shall I
go and call to thee a nurse of the Hebrew women, that she
may nurse the child for thee? And Pharaoh's daughter said
to her, Go. And the maid went and called the child's
mother. And Pharaoh's daughter said unto her, Take this
child away, and nurse it for me, and I will give thee thy
wages. And the woman took the child, and nursed it. And

the child grew, and she brought him unto Pharaoh's daughter, and he became her son. And she called his name Moses: and she said, Because I drew him out of the water."

As we can see from this story, Moses' sister watched as he was fished out of the water. She then came forth and asked the princess, "Shall I go and call to thee a nurse of the Hebrew women, that she may nurse the child for thee?" Pharaoh's daughter thought this was a great idea and sent the young lady on her way, not knowing that she'd just spoken with Moses' sister, and the woman who would be used to nurse Moses would be his very own mother. More than eighty years later, Moses would return to Egypt after having fled from the wrath of Pharaoh forty years prior, and he would be used by God to deliver God's people from the oppressive hands of Pharaoh. And while on their journey towards the Promised Land, Miriam, Moses' sister, would find herself questioning her brothers' authority. She would fantasize about removing him from his position of authority simply because he'd offended her by marrying an Ethiopian woman. Let's look at that particular story. Numbers 12:1–15 reads, "And Miriam and Aaron spake against Moses because of the Ethiopian woman whom he had married: for he had married an Ethiopian woman. And they said, Hath the LORD indeed spoken only by Moses? Hath he not spoken also by us? And the LORD heard it. (Now the man Moses was very meek, above all the men which were upon the face of the earth.) And the LORD spake suddenly unto Moses, and unto Aaron, and unto Miriam, Come out ye three unto the tabernacle of the congregation. And they three came out. And the LORD came down in the pillar of the cloud, and stood in the door of the tabernacle, and called Aaron and Miriam: and they both came forth. And he said, Hear now my words: If there be a prophet among you, I the LORD will make myself known unto him in a vision, and will speak unto him in a dream. My servant Moses is not so, who is faithful in all mine house. With him will I speak mouth to mouth, even apparently, and not in dark speeches; and the similitude of the LORD shall he behold: wherefore then were ye not afraid to speak against my servant Moses? And the anger of the LORD was kindled against them; and he departed. And the cloud departed from off the tabernacle; and, behold, Miriam became leprous, white as snow: and Aaron looked upon Miriam, and, behold, she was leprous. And Aaron said unto Moses, Alas, my lord, I beseech thee, lay not the sin upon us, wherein we have done foolishly, and wherein we have sinned. Let her not be as one dead, of whom the flesh is half consumed when he cometh out of his mother's womb. And Moses cried unto the LORD, saying, Heal her now, O God, I beseech thee. And the LORD said unto Moses, If her father had but spit in her face, should she not be ashamed seven days? Let her be shut out from the camp seven days, and after that let her be received in again. And Miriam was shut out from the camp seven days: and the people journeyed not till Miriam was brought in again."

Again, we're talking about relational protocol. What we witnessed with Miriam and Aaron is what we've come to know in the church as familiarity. Familiarity disregards rank and places everyone on a level plane. This may sound like a great idea until you see, for example, a war going on, and in the midst of a battlefield, you witness every soldier trying to take control, from the wisest soldier to the most emotional and unstable one. Rank is not a reward for service; it is the trust of a leader that we attain after we've proven our commitment through perseverance, loyalty, studying, and most of all, self-discipline. Nevertheless, there are people out there who don't feel like they should have to study in order to show themselves approved for the roles they desire to serve in and the seats they fantasize about sitting on. Please note that people like this are absolutely dangerous! They are the ones who create the most wars because of their lust for power and praise. Such was the case with Miriam. She was Moses' older sister, so more than likely, she didn't like being "bossed around" by her baby brother. And when he stepped outside of the invisible lines she'd placed around him, she saw her opportunity to rise up against him. We can see from the words that her and Aaron chose that they both wanted to rise to power. They'd said, "Hath the LORD indeed spoken only by Moses? Hath he not spoken also by us?" This lust for power led the two into the very crime that got Lucifer dubbed as Satan, demoted from his role as one of God's covering cherubs and evicted from Heaven. This is the crime of dishonor. Isaiah 14:12–15 reads, "How art thou fallen from heaven, O Lucifer, son of the morning! How art thou cut down to the ground, which didst weaken the nations! For thou hast said in thine heart, I will ascend into heaven, I will exalt my throne above the stars of God: I will sit also upon the mount of the congregation, in the sides of the north: I will ascend above the heights of the clouds; I will be like the most High. Yet thou shalt be brought down to hell, to the sides of the pit."

In the aforementioned story, we find the Most High God, YAWHEH, addressing Lucifer and his crimes against Him. He described the conversation that Lucifer had engaged in with himself. Lucifer had been a high-ranking angel; the Bible refers to him as a covering cherub. With rank comes a measure of access and knowledge, and according to 1 Corinthians 8:1, knowledge puffs up or, better yet, it makes people prideful. This is why God told us in Proverbs 4:7, "Wisdom is the principal thing; therefore get wisdom: and with all thy getting get understanding." We've all come in contact with pride-filled, religious people who promote their religion and their beliefs more than they promote the Most High God. They can talk for days about historical events and they can quote a lot of scriptures, but they are not wise, nor do they have understanding. Consequently, they become prideful, stubborn and idolatrous. Proverbs 16:18 says, "Pride goeth before destruction, and an haughty spirit before a fall." This is what happened with Miriam! But wait! Why did God punish Miriam and not Aaron? Think of it this way. Miriam and Aaron hadn't spoken simultaneously! All the same, her name was mentioned first in Numbers 12:1, which signifies that she was the first to speak up, inciting Aaron to rebel as well.

Miriam's crime against her brother mirrored the sin in which Lucifer committed when he incited a rebellion against God in Heaven. Because of his familiarity with God,

Lucifer fell into the trap of dishonor. Dishonor always makes people think that they can do their leaders' jobs better than their leaders. It makes children think that they are smarter than their parents. This is why we have to be careful with the thoughts we choose to entertain. Forbes Magazine reported the following:

> "According to the research of Dr. Fred Luskin of Stanford University, a human being has approximately 60,000 thoughts per day—and 90% of these are repetitive!" (Source: Forbes.com/Got Inner Peace? 5 Ways to Get it Now!/Christine Comaford).

Another news source reported that eighty percent of our thoughts are negative. Remember, Lucifer said in his heart what he'd intended to do, meaning he'd entertained a lot of evil thoughts. But those thoughts didn't get him in trouble. It was his subsequent behavior that cost him his role and his position. Revelation 12:7-9 reads, "And there was war in heaven: Michael and his angels fought against the dragon; and the dragon fought and his angels, and prevailed not; neither was their place found anymore in heaven. And the great dragon was cast out, that old serpent, called the Devil, and Satan, which deceiveth the whole world: he was cast out into the earth, and his angels were cast out with him." In other words, Lucifer became Satan, which means "adversary" when his thoughts graduated into actions. And this didn't happen the moment there was war in Heaven. This took place when he'd began speaking against YAHWEH to His angels. He led one-third of God's angels into an open rebellion, subsequently causing them to fall away from God. Revelation 12:3-4 reads, "And there appeared another wonder in heaven; and behold a great red dragon, having seven heads and ten horns, and seven crowns upon his heads. And his tail drew the third part of the stars of heaven, and did cast them to the earth: and the dragon stood before the woman which was ready to be delivered, for to devour her child as soon as it was born." The "stars of Heaven" referenced here are the angels of God. The dragon, of course, is Satan. Miriam's crime could have compromised God's plans for the Israelites. God had not appointed her to lead them, which meant that had she rose to power, she would have led the people astray.

Another example of familiarity and dishonor took place when Ham decided to expose his father. Let's look at their story. Genesis 9:20-27 reads, "And Noah began to be an husbandman, and he planted a vineyard: And he drank of the wine, and was drunken; and he was uncovered within his tent. And Ham, the father of Canaan, saw the nakedness of his father, and told his two brethren without. And Shem and Japheth took a garment, and laid it upon both their shoulders, and went backward, and covered the nakedness of their father; and their faces were backward, and they saw not their father's nakedness. And Noah awoke from his wine, and knew what his younger son had done unto him. And he said, Cursed be Canaan; a servant of servants shall he be unto his brethren. And he said, Blessed be the LORD God of Shem; and Canaan shall be his servant. God shall enlarge Japheth, and he shall dwell in the tents of Shem; and Canaan shall be his servant." Notice that Noah didn't curse Ham. In truth, he didn't speak a curse over Ham's lineage. He prophesied about the generational curse that would fall upon Ham's son, Canaan, and his ancestors as a result of Ham's decision. Why on Earth did Ham attempt to expose his father? This is a warfare tactic. Whenever a person wanted to usurp authority from another person, that individual would attempt to expose his leader's weaknesses. What do you think Lucifer did? Obviously, he couldn't find any weaknesses in God, so he fathered a system called "lies" in order to get God's angels to rebel against Him, and ultimately come under his control. Understand this—Lucifer was a high-ranking angel, and he understood the spirit realm more than most of the angels he led astray. Remember, with rank comes access to revelation! He knew that he would be losing his position since he was abdicating his role as a covering cherub, but he also knew that God's words cannot return to Him void, which meant that he would retain his rank. This meant that the angels that fell away with him would remain under his leadership! This would allow him to have the kingdom that he lusted after. What this means is that Lucifer usurped the authority of every angel he'd manipulated.

In truth, the word "familiarity" is now starting to have a negative stigma attached to it; this is because in order for a person to truly understand the concept and power of honor, that person would need to be brought up or raised up in a system of honor, otherwise, the concept of honor can sound relatively offensive. I think about the times when, as a teenager, I began to exhibit signs of familiarity towards my dad. I started becoming somewhat combative; I started pushing my limits with him. He let me get away with it for a short period of time. This only led me to push the envelope all the more. But one day, my dad decided to discipline me; this was something he rarely did. This served as a reminder to me that while he allowed me to joke around and play with him, he was still my father and I had to honor him as such. Of course, most children test their parents from time-to-time to see what they can and cannot get away with.

Another word for "familiarity" in the business world is "fraternization." The word "fraternize" is defined this way, "associate or form a friendship with someone, especially when one is not supposed to." I remember working in retail and hearing that term for the first time. Management was not allowed to fraternize with non-management. Doing so could get them fired. Nevertheless, a few of them didn't honor this rule, and in the majority of these cases, the employees became familiar with their managers. This led to some of them being inconsistent, combative or competitive. All the same, many of the managers in question feared disciplining the workers they'd fraternized with because—get this—many of the workers got close enough to the managers to know their weaknesses and their downfalls, and they began to use them against them. Some of the leaders ended up getting terminated because of their relationships with the hourly employees. One rule that most people in power understand is—to be careful that you don't allow anyone close who either doesn't have anything to lose or doesn't mind losing whatever it is that they have. The same rules apply in sororities, politics and all across the professional and relational spectrum, but it is only in the church that people tend to combat this the most.

Over time, I've learned the power of honor. No human taught me about honor. This was something God ministered to me about when I didn't have a church or a pastor, and thankfully, my parents instilled in me the understanding of honoring my elders and people in authority, regardless of whether I agreed with them or not. True honor is stable; it does not fail whenever we experience fear, offense or rejection. I can remember not having a church home and being taught by God about honor. Why was He teaching me this? Because God knew the doors that would open for me and the leaders He would place around me. Dishonor limits and/or annihilates a person's access to another person.

How does one move in honor, and what are the benefits of honor? To move in honor, simply respect the people who have been placed in authority, regardless of whether you like them or not or you agree with them or not. Romans 13:1-7 states, "Let every person be subject to the governing authorities. For there is no authority except from God, and those that exist have been instituted by God. Therefore whoever resists the authorities resists what God has appointed, and those who resist will incur judgment. For rulers are not a terror to good conduct, but to bad. Would you have no fear of the one who is in authority? Then do what is good, and you will receive his approval, for he is God's servant for your good. But if you do wrong, be afraid, for he does not bear the sword in vain. For he is the servant of God, an avenger who carries out God's wrath on the wrongdoer. Therefore one must be in subjection, not only to avoid God's wrath but also for the sake of conscience. For because of this, you also pay taxes, for the authorities are ministers of God, attending to this very thing. Pay to all what is owed to them: taxes to whom taxes are owed, revenue to whom revenue is owed, respect to whom respect is owed, honor to whom honor is owed." Notice the scripture says "every person," meaning no one is exempt from the law of honor. Again, every curse that ever sprouted in the Earth came as a result of dishonor.

To move in honor, you have to recognize your role and rank in every relationship and vice versa. For example, for some people, I am a leader and a mentor; then again, I also have leaders and mentors. This means that my roles and rank are not the same with everyone, and in order for me to extract the benefits and blessings from each relationship, I must first recognize and respect where I stand. Of course, I have to honor both the leaders and the people that I lead, but our relationships cannot and should not look the same.

Next, I must note that countries don't prepare for war in times of war; they prepare for war in times of peace. What does this mean? It's simple. I must fortify my heart by setting guidelines, rules, boundaries and establishing principles before I engage in any relationship, be it familial, platonic, corporate or romantic. For example, once God led me to my church home, I established a rule in my heart that I would not quit whenever things got tough, when I felt offended and whenever I felt overlooked, rejected or mishandled. I committed to remaining prayerful, only walking away should God tell me to do so. And get this—the season of offense hit me at one point, and it hit me hard! In truth, it was nearly unbearable! To make matters worse, it didn't lift for months! Everything in me wanted to walk away, but what anchored me in place was the commitment I'd made before I joined the church. During that season of offense, I repeatedly reminded myself of the commitment I'd made. I also increased in prayer. Additionally, I asked the Lord to give me wisdom and to show me where I was wrong. And when I felt overwhelmed to the point where I was ready to completely ignore the commitment, God gave me a dream, and in that dream, one of the leaders at my church saw me in an abortion clinic. He then walked over to me and asked what I was doing there. I tried to change the subject, but he interrupted with these words, "Let them crucify you." Now, this doesn't mean that people were hurting me; what I took this to mean was that my flesh was being killed and I needed to submit to the process. I posted the dream to Facebook, and here is how it read:

> "Let them crucify you." Those words will forever echo in my heart. Last night, I dreamed that, out of all places, I was in an abortion clinic. What's crazy is, I was happy to be there. I'd reasoned within myself that whatever it was that I was carrying, I didn't want it. I'd decided that I'd get it another way in another season under better conditions, but I didn't

want it at that moment. I was sitting across from a friend of mine, chatting away and laughing. We were both ready to throw away the fruit of our wombs just so that we could get our peace back. That's when my phone rang. It was a woman raving about a pastor I know and how he'd just preached fire at a funeral she'd attended. The funeral had taken place in another room at the abortion clinic. I told her how anointed he was and hung up. That's when I saw him leaving the clinic with his wife and children. I didn't bother to get his attention. I just pointed him out to my friend and turned back around. He went outside and was passing by the section we were seated in. There was a large window there and he glanced in and saw us. He then kissed his wife and asked her to wait in the car. He came back into the clinic, walked over and sat next to me. I greeted him and started telling him about the woman who'd just called me raving about his sermon. He wasn't interested in my small talk. He interrupted with, "What are you doing here?" I didn't answer. I just sat there. He then said, "Let them crucify you." In that dream, he made that statement three times because it was obvious that I'd made peace with the abortion. I'd made up my mind. After the final time, he said he had to leave but he reiterated, "Let them crucify you." I eventually left and went to another clinic, but I felt out of place since it was empty and left. After that, I woke up.

After sharing these words, I went on to encourage the people. I knew what the dream meant. God was answering the prayer that I'd lifted to Him many times in that season, and that prayer was about Him allowing me to church from home. Notice how I didn't bash my church or talk about my grievances. I used the dream to encourage others. The rest of the post reads:

> I've been having a series of dreams lately, but they were used by God to minister to me, but this one wasn't just for me. I believe it's for many of you. Obviously, I'm not with child cause I believe in, teach and exercise abstinence, so the pregnancy is spiritual. Notice I didn't dream that I was miscarrying, but rather that I was choosing to kill what was in me because I didn't like the situation I was in.
>
> Listen up. At this point, there will be no more miscarriages, meaning, you're going to choose whether you want to carry what's in you full term or if you want to abort it. If you choose to carry it, you are going to have to be crucified, meaning, you'll need to endure the stretching, the season you're in, and finally, the labor. The guy had to leave in the dream; he was nothing more than a ministering angel. His leaving meant he'd done his job. He wasn't going to hold my hand or coach me every step of the way. His job was to stop me from aborting what I was carrying. The same is true for you. In this season, you are gonna have to encourage yourself in the Lord; in this season, you will have to forgive while you're in the middle of

being crucified. Be encouraged and know that God is with you. He knows the beginning from the end. He has already gone ahead of you, defeated the enemy, and now He's letting you press through so that He can strengthen your faith. I'll reiterate to you what the angel of God said to me...let them crucify you.

Again, I was careful with my words, after all, I was hurting at that time. I'd just lost my mother to cancer seven months before that, and I felt like my life was crumbling before my eyes. To make matters worse, I was dealing with the spirit of offense, and that thing would not lift no matter how hard I fought it. Eventually, I came to realize that I needed wise counsel if I was going to get free. What's silly is the fact that I waited for so long to ask for help. I then prayed about who I could speak with because I didn't want to speak with someone who wrestled with gossip or someone who had an issue with the church because I wasn't looking for an alliance. I was genuinely looking for help. The Lord placed a woman on my heart who I knew to be extremely honorable, and after wrestling down pride, I finally reached out to her. This was one of the best decisions I'd made in that season because she listened to me cry it out and talk about my frustrations before ministering to me. She moved in absolute honor the entire time, and she prayed for me at the end of the call. Once we ended the call, I felt like a burden had been lifted. I was still feeling the hurt, but the heaviness was gone. Not long after that, I finally humbled myself enough to speak with my pastor about it. Of course, he ministered to me and that season eventually lifted. Nowadays, I'm glad I fought my way through it because I love my church and I know without a shadow of doubt that God placed me there. All the same, I am also super aware of how Satan fights covenant relationships.

And the third way to move in honor is to be honest. I'd made the mistake of hosting my hurt and offense for months. I kept trying to fight my way through it on my own, thinking that it would evaporate if I ignored it. I was wrong! It wasn't until I was honest with myself and honest with my leaders that I got free from that season.

Next, have conversations with the people you're disappointed with or hurt by, but before you do this, always make sure to dissect the issue and separate your wrongs from theirs. I call this process "sorting." Sorting, for me, is when I examine an issue from an objective standpoint and pull out the sordid details. I then take each offense or issue and determine who it belongs to. For example, let's create a character named Lucy. Let's say that Lucy and I went out to eat at Lucy's favorite restaurant for her birthday. I'd insisted on going somewhere else because the restaurant Lucy chose was extremely expensive. While this was going to be her birthday dinner, I didn't want to shell out a hundred bucks a plate! Nevertheless, Lucy insisted, stating that she'd pay for her own food. However, I knew that Lucy had absolutely no intentions of paying for her food. I knew her all too well! She knew that I would feel obligated to pay for her food since it was her birthday, and she knew that if I didn't pay for her food, I would be tormented by guilt. Regardless of this, we went out to Lucy's favorite spot, and she ordered the most expensive items on the menu! She ordered a rib-eye steak, mashed potatoes, and asparagus, and for dessert, she ordered the Crème Brûlée. Her ticket alone came out to be $174! My food totaled out to be $67. Once the waitress brought us our tickets, Lucy reached in her wallet to grab her debit card. I could see the offense on her face, after all, she's never been good at hiding her feelings! She wanted me to pay for her food! How disrespectful is that?! Finally, I pulled my card out of my wallet and said to the waitress, "I'm paying for both tickets." Lucy pretended to look shocked. "No, that's okay. I should have enough to cover my food," she said, all the while, pulling her card back towards her wallet. "No, I insist," I said in the most sarcastic of tones. When we left the restaurant, I was not only offended at how she'd manipulated me, but I was angry with myself for allowing her to manipulate me again. How would I dissect this situation?

First, I'd take accountability for my role in my own hurt and disappointment. Where did I go wrong?

1. I said I'd let her manipulate me again, suggesting that Lucy has a history of being manipulative. Clearly, I should have erected and established some boundaries long before this particular incident.

2. If I had offered to take Lucy out for her birthday, I should have had a budget in mind. If Lucy wanted to go to a super expensive restaurant, I should have said no. She could have gone to that restaurant on

her own and I could have taken her out another time.

3. If I'd given into her petition to take her out to her favorite restaurant, I should have given her a gift card to eat with. By doing this, I would be honoring her birthday, all the while, setting financial boundaries. For example, a $50 gift card to that restaurant would have been sufficient. If she went outside of that amount, the rest would be her own responsibility.

4. I should have ignored every temptation to pay for her dinner, and if that meant that she would walk away offended with me, I shouldn't have allowed this to negatively impact me.

5. It's clear that Lucy and I (if this were a true story) are not friends. Lucy is a consumer, and she's doing what consumers do—she's consuming! I would need to reevaluate our relationship and place the proper label on it. I'd then need to remove her from my intimate circle and see if I can find a place for her in my intellectual circle.

Lastly, I would need to surround myself with people who passionately believe in and practice honor. This would not only allow me to learn the language of honor, but it would help to establish a culture of honor in my life; this way, honor is no longer a job or something I have to remind myself to do, but instead, it would become instinctual.

What are the benefits of honor?
1. Unity.

2. The presence of God.
3. The favor of God.
4. The grace of God.
5. The peace of God.
6. The heart of God.
7. The plans of God.
8. The wisdom of God.
9. Supernatural wealth.
10. Healthy relationships.
11. Longstanding/lifelong relationships.
12. Blessings without sorrow.
13. Impartation.
14. Wholeness and healing.

Of course, there are more benefits because unity sets the temperature of an environment to the same temperature that we find in Heaven. This allows what's in Heaven to grow and flourish in the Earth.

Before I end this chapter, I must say this—the enemy of honor is dishonor (obviously), but the armor-bearer for dishonor is the spirit of offense. Easily offended people have a culture of dishonor because, get this—offense is an unclean spirit. This is why Proverbs 18:19 says, "A brother offended is harder to be won than a strong city: and their contentions are like the bars of a castle." To understand why this is, you have to have, at minimum, an elementary grasp of the layout of the soul. Jesus said in John 8:32, "And ye shall know the truth, and the truth shall make you free." In short, the spirit of offense is a guarding spirit. Without being too expansive, the soul is broken down into three realms; they are the mind, will and emotions. The first gate or the outer layer of the soul is the will. The center of the soul, also known as the heart, is the mind. The innermost part of the soul is the emotions. Most of the people who are within ear reach of us are there because we've willed them to be there. Sometimes, we have to allow people within our personal spaces because we work with them, worship with them, or live with them. Nevertheless, we choose where we work, we choose where we worship and we choose where we live and who we live with. This is our will. The information that we take in daily typically comes from the people within ear shot of us, the media, social media, our family and our friends. Everything we hear or see makes its way past our will; that is, unless we choose to ignore it and we allow into the outer courts of our minds. Our minds have three dimensions; they are the conscious, the subconscious and the unconscious. The conscious is the waiting room of the soul. This is where all of the information that we take in goes to be tested. If we don't believe a thread of information, our minds reject that information and it is cast out of our conscious. If it remains, it wears a tag of sorts. For example, when people say the Earth is flat, we may discard this information as false, but we'll remember that we've heard this statement before. This means that we'll quarantine the information. Whenever we come across information that we are unsure of, we'll normally leave that information in the conscious, pretty much storing it away for later use. Howbeit, whenever we decide that some information is true or we want it to be true, we come into agreement with it. This allows that information to make its way into the second level of our minds, which is the subconscious; this is the part of the mind that God told us to guard. The third level, also known as the unconscious mind, is the part of us that we have no control over. This is where our instincts lie, our greatest traumas are stored, our deepest memories are recorded, etc. Whenever a person gets saved, the unconscious becomes off-limits to the enemy, so he focuses all of his attention on the heart. This is why the Bible tells us to guard our hearts, stating that out of it (the heart) flows the issues of life.

The heart has many levels or states. They include the parental state, the daughter state, the financial state, the platonic state, the romantic state and the list goes on. Each of these states are in a certain condition, and some states border others. All the same, whatever we allow into our hearts creates a magnetic effect. How this works is, let's say that a person's heart is filled with lies. Satan will cause those lies to spread like a disease throughout every state of that person. Again, the goal is to build a siege wall around the spirit of that individual (if the person is saved). Whenever good information or truth is introduced to the conscious, the information that lives in the subconscious will war with the information in the conscious. This is why the Bible says that the truth shall set us free. Of course, demons will launch campaigns against the good information because they don't want to be dislodged. There are several guarding spirits, with the first one being fear and the second one being Leviathan (the king of pride). Leviathan twists the truth, making it hard for the recipient to understand the nature of the information or see God in it.

Instead, Leviathan makes the host think that the truth-teller is trying to take advantage of the individual, lying to the individual, wanting to control him or her, and the list goes on. This triggers the will of the individual, and this is where we find the spirit of offense lurking. This particular spirit comes forth to keep the truth out by causing the bound soul to partner with the enemy of his soul. This is spiritual Stockholm's Syndrome. I'm saying this to say—always choose to not be offended when you hear information that does not pair well with what you already believe. Simply pray about it, and then wait for God to respond in His timing! Also, study the Word of God so that you can find the answers there.

Trauma Bonds and Soul Ties

Let's start this chapter with a potent fact—when soul ties harden, they become yokes. Yokes are heavy and the burdens attached to them are cumbersome. This is why Jesus said, "Come unto me, all ye that labor and are heavy laden, and I will give you rest. Take my yoke upon you, and learn of me; for I am meek and lowly in heart: and ye shall find rest unto your souls. For my yoke is easy, and my burden is light" (Matthew 11:28-30). Since Jesus juxtaposed His meekness and lowliness with the weight of His yoke (which is light), we can safely assume that having relationships with prideful and haughty people is both burdensome and traumatic. What are the burdens that other people are carrying around? The answer is clear—the opinions, preferences, traumas and insecurities of other people. Think about it. On your first job, your issue was with a person, right? What about elementary, middle (grade) or high school? What about now? The problems that we face are people-centered. Then again, the Bible tells us that our war is not against flesh and blood, but against powers, principalities, the rulers of this dark world and spiritual wickedness in high places. This means that while we see and experience people hurting us, we've just touched the surface of the issue. We are spirits living in bodies, so it only makes sense that every issue we face is spiritual at its core. However, Satan cannot do the amount of damage that he wants to do to our hearts unless he gains intimate access to us through people. This is because, in order to fully operate in the Earth, you need a body. And this is where people and intimate relationships come in. Satan creates a siege of sorts around people by using other hurt people to hurt them. Before long, we look around and realize that we are surrounded on every side by people that we love, people who are hurting, traumatized, offended, rejected, and worst of all, they're looking for solutions outside of God. In other words, this sets the stage for them to reproduce their issues by placing demands on us that we cannot meet. When we are unable to fill those God-sized voids in their hearts, they respond by hurting us, and we, in turn, respond by hurting others. This is the domino effect of trauma that's been in motion since Eve first bit into the forbidden fruit. Soul ties are soft and beautiful in the beginning stages, but when they are ungodly, they soon turn into lassos, nooses, muzzles, whips, shackles and handcuffs.

Most leaders have come face-to-face with overly ambitious people who've tried to take over whatever it is that they were leading. Many of these leaders can tell stories of people they've put in positions of power, only to have those people turn the hearts of the people they were entrusted with away from the leader. Consider the story of Absalom. First, it all started with offense. His half-brother, Amnon, raped his sister, Tamar. Their father, David, didn't do anything about it. Was David wrong? Absolutely! But we have to understand that wrong doesn't necessarily mean disqualified. This is why there are so many people walking around dealing with a host of issues today, people who are in constant need of deliverance.

They focus on the sins, crimes and shortcomings of people in power, and rather than praying for their deliverance (see 1 Timothy 2:1-2) or restoring them with a spirit of meekness (see Galatians 6:1), they opt to open their mouths and speak against leaders whom God has anointed and appointed. Those who lust for power and recognition choose to bring their grievances to social media in hopes that by using the names of fallen or humiliated leaders, they too can grow their platforms. This luciferian mindset leads not only to dishonor and rebellion, but it also sets the stage for others to fall into the trap of dishonor, thus causing a split or divide in the body of Christ. 2 Samuel 15:1-12 details Absalom's crime. "And it came to pass after this, that Absalom prepared him chariots and horses, and fifty men to run before him. And Absalom rose up early, and stood beside the way of the gate: and it was so, that when any man that had a controversy came to the king for judgment, then Absalom called unto him, and said, Of what city art thou? And he said, Thy servant is of one of the tribes of Israel. And Absalom said unto him, See, thy matters are good and right; but there is no man deputed of the king to hear thee. Absalom said moreover, Oh that I were made judge in the land, that every man which hath any suit or cause might come unto me, and I would do him justice! And it was so, that when any man came nigh to him to do him obeisance, he put forth his hand, and took him, and kissed him. And on this manner did Absalom to all Israel that came to the king for judgment: so Absalom stole the hearts of the men of Israel.

And it came to pass after forty years, that Absalom said unto the king, I pray thee, let me go and pay my vow, which I have vowed unto the LORD, in Hebron. For thy servant vowed a vow while I abode at Geshur in Syria, saying, If the LORD shall bring me again indeed to Jerusalem, then I will serve the LORD. And the king said unto him, Go in peace. So he arose, and went to Hebron. But Absalom sent spies throughout all the tribes of Israel, saying, As soon as ye hear the sound of the trumpet, then ye shall say, Absalom reigneth in Hebron. And with Absalom went two hundred men out of Jerusalem, that were called; and they went in their simplicity, and they knew not any thing. And Absalom sent for Ahithophel the Gilonite, David's counseller, from his city, even from Giloh, while he offered sacrifices. And the conspiracy was strong; for the people increased continually with Absalom."

Notice that Absalom used his father, David's authority to garner access to the people David had been anointed to lead. This is what dishonorable people do. They use their access to a person in authority to access and manipulate the people they've been entrusted with. They don't always say something bad about their leaders. Instead, I've come to find that they tend to do the opposite. They speak well about the leaders for a while, but their hearts are dark towards their leaders. Slowly but surely, they create soul ties with the people under their care, and once these soul ties are created, they then start playing the victim. For example, they may say, "The Lord has placed it upon my heart to leave this church, but hey! Don't you guys leave! Honor our pastor, after all, he is truly anointed by God! But God has been giving me one dream after the other telling me to get out of there." Notice that the person demonstrated false honor by saying that the pastor is truly anointed, and then telling the people not to leave. But the individual in question also eluded to the church being ungodly by saying that the Lord has told him or her to "get out of there."

Absalom's lust for power would continue to grow until he'd split Israel in half. 2 Samuel 16:15-23 reads, "And Absalom, and all the people the men of Israel, came to Jerusalem, and Ahithophel with him. And it came to pass, when Hushai the Archite, David's friend, was come unto Absalom, that Hushai said unto Absalom, God save the king, God save the king. And Absalom said to Hushai, Is this thy kindness to thy friend? Why wentest thou not with thy friend? And Hushai said unto Absalom, Nay; but whom the LORD, and this people, and all the men of Israel, choose, his will I be, and with him will I abide. And again, whom should I serve? Should I not serve in the presence of his son? As I have served in thy father's presence, so will I be in thy presence. Then said Absalom to Ahithophel, Give counsel among you what we shall do. And Ahithophel said unto Absalom, Go in unto thy father's concubines, which he hath left to keep the house; and all Israel shall hear that thou art abhorred of thy father: then shall the hands of all that are with thee be strong. So they spread Absalom a tent upon the top of the house; and Absalom went in unto his father's concubines in the sight of all Israel. And the counsel of Ahithophel, which he counselled in those days, was as if a man had inquired at the oracle of God: so was all the counsel of Ahithophel both with David and with Absalom."

Notice how the conspiracy revealed who David's true friends were. This is why God gave us the mechanism of will. And please note that willpower is not power unless we have something to choose from! Lucifer discovered that he had a choice; he could continue following God, allowing YAHWEH to use him as an instrument of worship, or he could blaze his own trail. He chose the latter, but with every choice comes consequences.

As a leader, it can be frustrating whenever I launch a program, only to find emails from offended people who demand refunds simply because I won't allow them to get as close to me as they want to. Instead, they find boundaries and systems in place that allow me to teach them without always creating the types of soul ties they want to create. The average believer thinks that they need to talk to their leaders so that the leaders can customize or tailor their leadership to them. This belief stems from one of the most common demonic attacks that Satan launches against the mind. Satan simply plants a seed in the hearts of people called self-sabotage. Self-sabotage starts off as a small voice that does not overpower the voices of the people; it is subtle and relatively non-invasive. This voice says, "No one can understand you" or "Your situation is different than everyone else's." This causes people to believe that while the Bible is true and infallible, the entirety of the Bible is not applicable to their lives and their situations because of:

1. What they've experienced.
2. Their own good intentions.
3. What others have told them.

This causes people to think that they don't just need to sit in the congregation; they need to have a personal one-on-one conversation with the pastor himself or herself to explain their unique situations. Again, while it is unspoken, they've somehow come to believe that they are exempt from some laws or principles listed in the Bible; this is simply because Satan has managed to convince them that no one else has ever experienced what they have experienced or are experiencing. This attitude sets the stage for the spirit of offense to come in. Think about Bishop T.D. Jakes' church. It is impossible for him to sit down and talk with every single congregant or visitor there! After all, everyone would require, at minimum, one hour of his time, and more than ninety percent of those people would want to have a series of follow-up conversations. This is why Jethro instructed Moses to appoint leaders to help him with the people. Every person likely felt that their situation was different and more important than every other individuals' situation. So, they stood in line waiting for their turns to speak with Moses. Bishop Jakes has leaders in place, just as Moses had to appoint leaders. But there are people who absolutely hate megachurches because they want to have one-on-one, up close and personal relationships with their leaders, and while there is nothing inherently wrong with this, we have to ask ourselves why we feel this way if we should find ourselves desiring to be close to our leaders. Howbeit, the truth is that a lot of people are in need of deliverance; we know this, so their desires to get close to leaders are oftentimes demonically centered. How can I say this with a straight face? Because I'm a leader who knows leaders, and we've witnessed what happens whenever people rush and push themselves upon leaders. They typically don't understand rank, protocol or honor. Consequently, they become familiar with their leaders way too fast, and one day, they say in their hearts, "I can do his job better than him" or "I can preach better than her!" After this, they begin to speak with others within that church or organization, turning the hearts of those people away from the leaders. People like this are oftentimes narcissistic and controlling, which is why they are in a hurry to create soul ties with their leaders and many of the people under those leaders. Think about the classic narcissist. One red flag or symptom of narcissism is what the world of psychology refers to as "love bombing." Very Well Mind reports the following:

"'Many people who love bomb are narcissists who are looking to control their victim,' Huynh said. They form a close bond quickly, often choosing people who have codependent tendencies, or who seem vulnerable and inviting of a 'savior.' Then, they will start to take control once they know there is an attachment. But it's important to remember that not all people who love bomb have NPD, Steele said. Sometimes love bombing comes from a place of unresolved pain and conflict. Our attachment style—which describes behavior patterns in relationships—and how conscious we are of it, can drive us. For example, someone with an insecure attachment style may love bomb in an effort to "secure" the relationship quickly, out of fear the partner will abandon them. The problem is, love bombing may overwhelm a partner and push them away, leading to a sort of self-fulfilling prophecy" (Source: Very Well Mind/Is It Love or Love-Bombing?/Sarah Simon).

Notice that the author of the article said that narcissists would start to take control once they know that there is an attachment. The attachment in question is what we refer to in the church as a soul tie. Narcissists specialize in creating soul ties with others; this is why they are oftentimes in a rush to get close to not just leaders but any person they feel can appease a lust, need or desire that they have. The author also noted that not everyone who love bombs is a narcissist, however, love-bombing is a sign of unresolved pain and conflict. In other words, a lot of the people in question are accustomed to forming trauma bonds with people. Trauma bonds are soul ties that are centered around trauma. Psychology Today reports the following about trauma bonding:

"Trauma-bonding lives in the nervous system. The brain makes associations between "love" and abuse or neglect.

- Trauma-bonding is a hormonal attachment created by repeated abuse, sprinkled with being "saved" every now and then.
- Trauma-bonding in adulthood can stem from childhood trauma" (Source: Psychology Today/What is Trauma Bonding?/A Personal Perspective: Why You Keep Choosing Unavailable or Abusive Partners/Ingrid Clayton, Ph.D.)

Most people think that trauma bonding is only defined by

how abusers or narcissists get people to soul tie themselves to them, but it goes much further and deeper than that. It is a system of creating relationships as a result of past or present traumas. The goal of the individual seeking to create the bond is to traumatize another person and then come to the rescue. In short, people who have been abused and traumatized by narcissists and/or abusers also learn to specialize in trauma-bonding themselves to others. How does this look? In my experience, what people typically do is they'll look for a need in a leader or a person's life. For example, let's create a character named Janice. Janice follows a pastor online and eventually decides that she wants to be a part of his church. She visits the church, and the experience is better than amazing! Janice joins the church, but because she's overly determined to get close to the pastor, she immediately starts looking for a place to volunteer. Volunteering is awesome, but we have to have the right intentions. Janice's intentions are not pure. She's desperately in search of affirmation and she doesn't want to shell out a hundred bucks a session to a therapist, so she often fantasizes about sitting down with the pastor to tell him about her life, her God-given gifts and all the dreams she's had over the last few years. She volunteers to work in the church's cafe, but soon enough, she discovers that her position doesn't give her the type of access to the pastor she wants. So, she volunteers with the cleaning team; she reasons that this would give her access to the pastor's office, and over time, she will bump into him. Janice believes that once the pastor sees her and hears her story, he will want to walk close with her. She puts a lot of heart and passion into cleaning the church, especially the pastor's office. She even takes the time out to organize his desk, creating a system that makes it easier for him to find his notes. The pastor greets and thanks to Janice for being so detailed and excellent in all that she does. This excites Janice, but the pastor immediately leaves after this because he has another event to get to. Janice increases her workload. She organizes everything in the pastor's office, even taking the time out to iron the clothes he has hanging in his makeshift closet. She creates a standard of excellence that none of the other women can attain or maintain, making herself a pivotal fixture in that particular ministry. And then, without warning, Janice simply does not show up at church one Sunday. She sits by her phone, waiting to see if anyone is going to call and check on her. Only one person calls; that is Ms. Jones, but Janice does not answer her call. She listens to Ms. Jones' voice mail, but Janice believes that the pastor himself should reach out to her. This doesn't happen because the pastor has people in place to help him with these types of issues so that he is not overwhelmed. Offended, Janice shows back up to church four weeks later, but she does not volunteer. Instead, she sits in the congregation, hoping to be noticed. She's greeted by a lot of the people who are familiar with her, but no one stops to address her absence. That following Tuesday, Janice returns during Bible study and starts cleaning the church again. She says to Ms. Jones, "I was not feeling well. That's why I was absent." But deep in her heart, she questions why no one outside of Ms. Jones called to check on her. What was Janice doing? She was attempting to create a trauma bond by creating a demand, and then suddenly leaving that demand unmet. You'd be amazed at how common this behavior is; ask any leader! Had she gotten as close to the leader as she wanted to get, she would have hurt him or attempted to hurt him the moment she got offended, and get this—Janice is easily offended! Why do people do this? Because it works! It brings people to their mercy. If the pastor had responded the way Janice wanted him to respond, he would have called her to find out why she's been missing church. Janice would have utilized that opportunity to detail her grievances to the pastor or, better yet, test to see how much leverage or control she has over him. She may say something like, "I haven't been feeling well; that's why I didn't come, but all the same, I've been thinking about resigning lately because I feel like I need more one-on-one mentorship. I've been dealing with a lot of warfare, starting with my narcissistic mother, my oldest son and my ex-husband, and I feel alone in the issue." In other words, she's trying to force the pastor to minister to her about her personal issues. Isn't this what pastors do? Not really. Pastors have an entire congregation to lead. Sure, you can set up pastoral counseling sessions with most pastors, but they can't offer extensive counseling to you. Instead, most pastors will refer you to a therapist. This is to say that our pastors can't serve as our personal therapists, nor are they our parents.

Again, bound people hate boundaries with an undying passion! All the same, bound people try to bind other people to a bunch of rules, unrealistic expectations and limitations. I always try to explain to my students that I am not a replacement for God, nor can I serve as an idol. Nevertheless, I do understand the fears that some of them have. They've dealt heavily with rejection and abandonment, and they genuinely believe that if they don't get close to their leaders fast, they will be overlooked and rejected. So, they rush to create soul ties with me and some of the other students, only to come face-to-face with a set of boundaries. Thankfully, I'm able to help most of them to understand that they are not being rejected. Something my pastor preached during one Sunday service changed my perspective about relationships, especially corporate ones. He said, "If you're called to me, what's the rush?" I thought about it and the light came on in my heart. Every good and Godly relationship doesn't have to be rushed, nor should it ever be rushed. Rushed relationships tend to end fast and they tend to be toxic and messy!

Narcissist Magnets

Are you a narcissist magnet? If so, you are in good company. And like most people who've repeatedly found themselves entangled with narcissistic folks, you've likely wondered why these types of people are attracted to you, or what's worse, why you are attracted to them. There's a natural and spiritual science behind this, and by the time you finish reading this chapter, you will understand why, to narcissists, you seem to stand out in a crowd. But first, let's take a closer look at the topic of narcissism.

What is narcissism? The following article was taken from Mayo Clinic:

> "Narcissistic personality disorder — one of several types of personality disorders — is a mental condition in which people have an inflated sense of their own importance, a deep need for excessive attention and admiration, troubled relationships, and a lack of empathy for others. But behind this mask of extreme confidence lies a fragile self-esteem that's vulnerable to the slightest criticism. A narcissistic personality disorder causes problems in many areas of life, such as relationships, work, school or financial affairs. People with narcissistic personality disorder may be generally unhappy and disappointed when they're not given the special favors or admiration they believe they deserve. They may find their relationships unfulfilling, and

others may not enjoy being around them.

Signs and symptoms of narcissistic personality disorder and the severity of symptoms vary. People with the disorder can:

- Have an exaggerated sense of self-importance.
- Have a sense of entitlement and require constant, excessive admiration.
- Expect to be recognized as superior even without achievements that warrant it.
- Exaggerate achievements and talents.
- Be preoccupied with fantasies about success, power, brilliance, beauty or the perfect mate.
- Believe they are superior and can only associate with equally special people.
- Monopolize conversations and belittle or look down on people they perceive as inferior.
- Expect special favors and unquestioning compliance with their expectations.
- Take advantage of others to get what they want.
- Have an inability or unwillingness to recognize the needs and feelings of others.
- Be envious of others and believe others envy them.
- Behave in an arrogant or haughty manner, coming across as conceited, boastful and pretentious.
- Insist on having the best of everything — for instance, the best car or office.

At the same time, people with narcissistic

personality disorder have trouble handling anything they perceive as criticism, and they can:

- Become impatient or angry when they don't receive special treatment.
- Have significant interpersonal problems and easily feel slighted.
- React with rage or contempt and try to belittle the other person to make themselves appear superior.
- Have difficulty regulating emotions and behavior.
- Experience major problems dealing with stress and adapting to change.
- Feel depressed and moody because they fall short of perfection.
- Have secret feelings of insecurity, shame, vulnerability and humiliation".
  (Source: Mayo Clinic/Narcissistic Personality Disorder).

What if I told you that what the world of psychology refers to as the narcissist is what the church has been referring to as the Jezebel spirit for centuries? The Bible tells us that there is nothing new under the sun, and we can truly see this in the many practices that are being popularized by the New Age Movement and other pagan movements. What many of them do is take Christian laws and principles, and then repackage them. For example, the concept of karma, found in the Hindu religion, is just a repackaged and relabeled version of sowing and reaping. And we see this concept by popularized by New Agers as well. Galatians 6:7 reads, "Be not deceived; God is not mocked: for whatsoever a man soweth, that shall he also reap." This is the Word of God, therefore it is a law. This means that it is absolute; it has no choice but to come to pass. And now, we hear a lot of nonbelievers and believers alike talking about karma when, in truth, there is no karma, only the law of sowing and reaping. Let's look at some characteristics of the Jezebel spirit. People who have this wicked spirit:

1. Refuse to admit guilt or wrongdoing; will not repent.
2. Will often project the blame onto someone else or, at minimum, share the blame with someone else.
3. Have a grandiose sense of importance.
4. Tend to pursue people in power, but they will either ignore or be rather condescending towards people they feel are insignificant.
5. Tend to withhold information so that they can remain superior or appear to be more knowledgeable and valuable than their co-workers and counterparts.
6. Weaponize the spirit of confusion to control conversations and narratives.
7. Love to use the names of powerful people to manipulate, dominate and seduce others.
8. Are controlling (either overtly or covertly).
9. Have trouble submitting to authority.
10. Hate and will often rebel against rules.
11. Love to take credit for anything and everything.
12. Tend to use people to accomplish their agenda.
13. Wrestle with jealousy; are very competitive.
14. Are very critical of others.

15. Weaponize their tears to get what they want.
16. Use flying monkeys to dominate and bully others into giving them what they want.
17. Must be the center of attention.
18. Use flattery and gifts to gain access to powerful people.
19. Are oftentimes clairvoyant.
20. Are vengeful.
21. Are incredibly ambitious.
22. Will sequester information to later use it against others.
23. Tend to volunteer for everything in an attempt to be recognized, promoted and empowered.
24. Tend to use generalization (think isms) to promote hatred and division.
25. Are known to split or damage churches and religious movements.

Did you notice the similarities between the Jezebel spirit and what the world of psychology refers to as the narcissist? They are one and the same! Also, consider this—there is a spectrum for everything that is classified as descriptive. For example, good cannot be good unless evil exists, tall cannot be tall unless short exists, and east can only exist if there is a west. I'm saying that to say this—on the Christian spectrum, we know that whenever and wherever you find Jezebel, you will also find Ahab. All the same, in the secular world, wherever and whenever you find a narcissist, there has to be something on the other end of that spectrum. The world of psychology and many pagan movements have dubbed this character as the empath. This is important because the church at large has accepted the concept of the narcissist, and this wicked character is being preached about in pulpits around the world. Many leaders even recognize the narcissist as the Jezebel spirit, which is great! But if you use the word "empath" in many Christian establishments, you will invoke the wrath of the religious. This is because the word "empath" has been popularized by the New Age movement, even though it did not originate there.

At the end of 2020, the Lord impressed upon my heart to create some messages on YouTube and use the word "empath." The goal was to get the attention of some of the people who were either a part of the New Age movement or people who identified with many of their beliefs. In other words, the Lord told me to go out into the world in language. I did just that. Sure enough, many witches and unbelievers came to my channel in droves and got saved. All the same, many people who were already saved, yet dabbling in New Age practices repented and turned their lives around. All it took was for me to speak their language. Did I get any backlash? Yes indeed! It was then that I truly came to understand why God detests religion so much. Here's what the Lord taught me:

1. Most people who identify themselves as empaths are prophets and prophetic people.
2. One of the characteristics of empaths is that they're super sensitive. In truth, their sensitivity is from God. As prophets and prophetic people, they were created to be sensitive to God's presence; this is what allows them to feel inspired , feel the

anointing and to be as creative as they are. (Note: there are degrees of creativity; the more creative a person is, the more prophetic and sensitive that person will likely be).

3. Many empaths (prophets, prophetic people), because of their super sensitivity, wrestle with fear, and it is this fear that sets the stage for the narcissist (Jezebel spirit) to enter their lives.

4. Jezebel loves untapped authority. What this means is that we all have a measure of authority, but whenever we don't do what God told us to do because of fear and intimidation, we lay that authority by the wayside. This is how prophets and prophetic people pick up the Ahab spirit. And when a person is bound by Ahab, that person will automatically attract Jezebel (the narcissist) into his or her life. This is because Jezebel and Ahab are married in the realm of the spirit!

5. Prophets like to hide; they hide in congregations, religious churches that don't believe they exist, relationships, jobs and wherever they can blend in, but like Jonah, they often find themselves consumed by a great fish. This great fish is Jezebel. This is why it is difficult to cast Jezebel out of the prophet; instead, you have to coach the prophet out of Jezebel. After all, Jezebel isn't just a demon, it's a principality and a system; it's a way of doing things!

6. Idolatry is the enemy of the empath/prophetic person. It is the perfume that attracts the narcissist/Jezebel to the prophetic person. Narcissists will only stay where they're tolerated

and worshiped! "Notwithstanding I have a few things against thee, because thou sufferest that woman Jezebel, which calleth herself a prophetess, to teach and to seduce my servants to commit fornication, and to eat things sacrificed unto idols" (Revelation 2:20).

7. Prophetic people spend a great deal of time tolerating this spirit, and then breaking up with the people who are bound by it, but many never get fully free because the key to their deliverance is repentance! Jonah had to repent for running from his assignment in the belly of the great fish! And repentance is more than just apologizing to God; it's more than finally saying "no" to the devil. It's also saying "yes" to God! If you reject the devil but you don't accept the will of God for your life, you put your purpose in park.

Narcissists are attracted to prophets and prophetic gifts who are:
1. Broken; traumatized.
2. Unaware of who they are.
3. Toxic.
4. Powerful.
5. Anointed.
6. Unguarded.
7. Idolatrous.
8. Living in isolation.
9. Fearful.
10. Lust driven.

One of the ways to keep yourself safe from a narcissist's advances is to simply say "yes" to God. Additionally, stay within the confines of God's will. You see, Satan needs a sin offering to legally operate in your life. This is why narcissists and toxic people use love-bombing, flattery and gifts in their attempts to rush you into a soul tie with them. They try to skip Circle 5 and rush right into Circle 1, and if you allow them to do this, you will experience the effects of euphoria. And while this is a great feeling, this feeling sets the stage for addiction; this addiction is what we call idolatry. This is the same effect that drugs have on the human body. Check out the following article:

> "Cocaine produces its psychoactive and addictive effects primarily by acting on the brain's limbic system, a set of interconnected regions that regulate pleasure and motivation. An initial, short-term effect—a buildup of the neurochemical dopamine—gives rise to euphoria and a desire to take the drug again" (National Library of Medicine/The Neurobiology of Cocaine Addiction/Eric J. Nestler, M.D., Ph.D.).

The following snippet was taken from a paper written by Heather M. Chapman for University of Rhode Island:

> "In order to understand the brain's response to love, one must examine the brain and fully comprehend the myriad array of structures involved. One of the main structures involved with falling in love is the limbic system. The particular system is well known as being the part of the brain involved in emotional response. The limbic system is actually several

structures combined, including the basal nuclei, the thalamus, and the hypothalamus. While all of these structures are vital, the hypothalamus is directly involved in both behavioral and sexual function. Combining these two important functions, one can see how the limbic system is so crucial to falling in love" (Source: University of Rhode Island/DigitalCommons@URI/Love: A Biological, Psychological and Philosophical Study/Heather M. Chapman).

This proves that falling in love has the same effect on your brain as drugs. This is one of the greatest and most effective campaigns Satan has ever launched! Most westerners are addicted to the effects of falling in love. Consequently, most westerners do not test the spirits in the people they decide to befriend, date, court or marry! If this isn't bad enough, just imagine what effect this has on the super-sensitive prophet or prophetic person! Let's add another layer to this! Imagine what effect this has on the super-sensitive prophet or prophetic person who has an unguarded heart, trauma and that vicious black hole that we call a void! Let's add another layer to this—now place that prophet or prophetic person in a relationship with Jezebel for five or more years. This is why there are so many prophets and prophetic people locked away in mental hospitals. By the time Jezebel is done with that soul, the person ends up needing more deliverance than Jezebel does! And yes, the Jezebel spirit can be in men as well!

Are you a prophet or a prophetic person? Below, I've listed

a few characteristics of prophets and prophetic people, but do not attempt to call or activate yourself. Get into a good church home, and God will confirm your calling, not just to you but through others.

Signs That You May be a Prophet or a Prophetic Person
1. You're creative. God is the Creator, we are His creations, and therefore, we are creative. Creativity has nothing to do with your abilities and everything to do with how you're wired. Super creative people are typically very prophetic.
2. You have vivid dreams that come to pass.
3. You have or have had visions that have come to pass.
4. You are incredibly sensitive; the more sensitive you are, the more likely you are to isolate yourself from the world.
5. You can sometimes feel the emotions of others.
6. You love or are drawn to intercessory prayer.
7. You have an incredible passion for people; this love causes you to want to help people. It has also gotten you in trouble because you've tried to help the wrong people and ended up getting traumatized as a result.
8. Your peace goes completely out the window in chaotic atmospheres. You absolutely need an atmosphere of peace to function.
9. You fall in love easily.
10. You often pray prophetically.
11. You have an unquenchable desire to get closer to God, and no matter how close you get to Him, it

never feels like you're close enough!
12. You're a narcissist magnet.

Next, how do you break the cycle of narcissistic abuse in your life?

1. You have to divorce that spirit! You do this by taking back all of your authority from it and obeying God. In other words, do what God told you to do repeatedly.

2. Heal. Narcissists love soul tying and then trauma bonding themselves to bleeding prophets. Get a therapist and commit to returning to that therapist until you've fully healed.

3. Don't date until you heal! When you're broken, your judgment is cloudy, and chances are, the people that you're attracted to are representatives of your old season.

4. Mature in Christ. You do this by studying the Word of God daily, showing up at church (this includes Bible Study) and being intentional about exercising your faith.

5. Don't rush into a relationship with anyone! Let each person go through the process and earn their way into your intimate space.

6. Don't forget your wise counsel! Be accountable, be honest and be willing to walk away if your wise counsel points out some obvious red flags about your love interest.

7. No sex! No sex! No sex! Save it for marriage!

8. Test the spirit from the start! If someone expresses interest in you, ask the person if he or she is saved.

Ask the individual what church he or she goes to. Remember, the Bible says not to be unequally yoked with unbelievers (see 2 Corinthians 6:14).

9. Don't ignore the red flags!

10. Don't allow yourself to be love-bombed! Keep all communications above the surface.

11. Pray about everything and everyone! I've done this for many years now, and it has saved my life!

12. Look at the fruits of the Spirit versus the works of the flesh in the person's life. Which of these are prevalent in that person's life? Which one of these gardens does he or she tend to the most?

13. Get regular bouts of deliverance. It's okay. We all have to eat our daily bread.

14. Let people go! It may hurt, but in the long run, it works out for your better and maybe even for their betterment as well.

15. Seek the Kingdom of God first; put God first in all things. You do this through prayer, fasting and meditating on His Word.

16. Say "yes" to your Godly assignment before you say "yes" to a relationship.

17. Don't allow anyone to control you. Your authority is linked to your authenticity. Don't lose yourself in Jezebel.

18. Never tolerate Jezebel. "Notwithstanding I have a few things against thee, because thou sufferest that woman Jezebel, which calleth herself a prophetess, to teach and to seduce my servants to commit fornication, and to eat things sacrificed unto idols" (Revelation 2:20).

19. When someone shows you who are they, believe them and act accordingly.
20. Invest or sow your time into things that are productive; this way, you won't waste your time entertaining narcissists.

You may be a Jezebel or a narcissist magnet, but you can learn to repel that spirit just by forgiving others, serving God, setting boundaries and refusing to settle for less than what you're worth. And if you don't know how valuable you are, please find a therapist so that you can rebuild your mind. You got this!

TESTING THE SPIRIT

1 John 4:1 reads, "Beloved, believe not every spirit, but try the spirits whether they are of God: because many false prophets are gone out into the world." What does it mean to test a spirit? After all, most of us are intellectually familiar with this particular scripture, but we're not intimately familiar with it. To test a spirit, the first thing you have to familiarize yourself with is the Word of God. A lot of people want the power of God (ex: discernment, the ability to cast out devils, the gift of prophecy) without studying the Word of God, and this has led so many believers into witchcraft. So again, first and foremost, you have to study God's Word. 2 Timothy 2:15 states, "Study to shew thyself approved unto God, a workman that needeth not to be ashamed, rightly dividing the word of truth." What are we being approved for? God answers this question in Hosea 4:6; it reads, "My people are destroyed for lack of knowledge: because thou hast rejected knowledge, I will also reject thee, that thou shalt be no priest to me: seeing thou hast forgotten the law of thy God, I will also forget thy children." In short, we study to acquire knowledge; this way, we can become the priests of God. But what exactly does this mean? Of course, God was not and is not referring to the Levitical priesthood, but to understand this, we have to look at a couple of the benefits that Levitical priests had, and one of those benefits was the ability to draw near God. Levitical priests had an access to God that no ordinary man or woman had.

This also meant that they had access to wisdom, knowledge and revelation, making them wiser than the average person. They were able to discern between what was holy versus unholy. So, in this, God is saying that people who reject knowledge won't have the intimate access to Him that others who embrace knowledge have. Of course, Jesus is our High Priest, and we are all now able to go into the presence of God, but remember, God's presence doesn't automatically equate to God's approval. James 4:8 says, "Draw nigh to God, and he will draw nigh to you. Cleanse your hands, ye sinners; and purify your hearts, ye double minded." How do we draw nigh or near to God? Psalm 145:48 reads, "The LORD is nigh unto all them that call upon him, to all that call upon him in truth." We call upon Him, but understand that calling upon Him is not just saying, whispering or shouting His name. He said that we must call upon Him in truth. Psalm 119:160 reads, "Thy word is true from the beginning: and every one of thy righteous judgments endureth for ever." If the Word is true or truth, and according to John 14:16, Jesus is Truth, this could only mean that we have to know the Word, but knowing the Word denotes intimacy. It is far more than just quoting scriptures. This happens when we take the Word of God from our intellect and store it in our hearts. Our hearts are our personal gardens; when the Word is in our hearts, we begin to bear the fruits of the Spirit. But when the Word is not in our hearts, we will be filled with voids, and as we discussed earlier, voids are dark spots or dark rooms in the soul. What happens in darkness? Mildew, mold and other bacteria flourishes! In our cases, the works of the flesh will flourish wherever there is no light (revelation). This means that to test a spirit, we must know the Word, and we must also know the differences between the fruits of the Spirit versus the works of the flesh. Let's look at them both.

- **Works of the Flesh (Galatians 5:19-21):** Now the works of the flesh are manifest, which are these; Adultery, fornication, uncleanness, lasciviousness, idolatry, witchcraft, hatred, variance, emulations, wrath, strife, seditions, heresies, envyings, murders, of which drunkenness, revellings, and such like: I tell you before, as I have also told you in time past, that they which do such things shall not inherit the kingdom of God.
- **Fruits of the Spirit (Galatians 5:22-23):** But the fruit of the Spirit is love, joy, peace, longsuffering, gentleness, goodness, faith, meekness, temperance: against such there is no law.

Of course, in order to see many of these fruits, you need time. Narcissists and toxic people specialize in creating soul ties with people by accelerating the pace of a relationship through a process called "love bombing." We spoke briefly about love-bombing earlier, but let's get a clearer definition of this. Psychology Today reports the following:

"Love bombing is the practice of overwhelming someone with signs of adoration and attraction — think flattering comments, tokens of affection, or love notes on the mirror, kitchen table, or windshield, and you're beginning to get the picture. It's flowers delivered at work with hearts dotting the i's in your name. It's texts that increase in frequency as they increase in romantic fervor. It's surprise appearances designed to manipulate you into spending more time with the bomber — and, not coincidentally, less time with others, or on your own" (Source: Psychology Today/Love Bombing: A Narcissist's Secret Weapon/Suzanne Degges-White Ph.D.)

Choosing Therapy had this to say about love-bombing:
"Love bombing essentially means continuously "bombing" your relational partner with flattery, compliments, and affections. This attention can come in various forms: gifts, long-winded messages, social media interactions, and passionate declarations of love. However, love bombing isn't purely altruistic. People use love bombing because they also want to feel praised and adored. Therefore, they will lavish their partners hoping that their partners will return the favor.
Interestingly, love bombing doesn't just have its roots in romantic relationships. Research shows that cult leaders often employ these tactics to attract and retain members. Subsequently, even if a member leaves the cult, they often feel riddled with guilt, fear, and uncertainty regarding whether or not they've made the right decision – a hallmark of religious trauma. In addition, the same love bombing tactics may be used in other forms of psychological manipulation, such as with pimps, gang leaders, or toxic leaders" (Source: Choosing

Therapy/Love Bombing: Definition, Signs, & What to Do/Nicole Arzt, LMFT).

What this essentially means for you is that you have to be mindful of the connections you create with people. To do this, you must set boundaries. Don't allow people to rush you into relationships or to obligate you to roles or responsibilities in their lives that God has not approved you for. This means that you have to be prayerful about everyone. All the same, don't allow people to tell you who they are to you. Over the course of time, you should be able to see their fruits or their works and determine what roles, if any, they can play in your life, and vice versa.

CRABS IN A BUCKET

If you've lived long enough, chances are, you've heard the phrase "crabs in a bucket," otherwise known as "crab mentality" or "herd behavior." Psychology Today published the following article about this mindset:

"Do you feel like others are holding you back? This has come to be called "the crab bucket syndrome" because crabs pull back those who try to escape. A lone crab can climb out of a bucket, but when its mates are present, it ends up boiled to death with them.

Maybe you feel like this is happening to you—whether family or friends or coworkers; whether actively undermining you or just failing to applaud when you think you deserve it. Sometimes you even feel pushed to choose between escaping the bucket and preserving your social bonds.

Crabs did not evolve in buckets. They evolved on seashores, where clinging to others promoted survival. A crab is not consciously trying to hold back its mates. It is not consciously trying to save them either. It is just repeating a behavior that was naturally selected for" (Source: Psychology Today/When Others Hold You Back/Loretta G. Breuning Ph.D.).

Earlier on, we talked about consumers versus producers. Understand this—a season is not a space of time that we find ourselves locked in. While there is a time element to seasons, a season is a mindset that you are locked into for a space of time. Your mindset will determine who you walk with, what you have, what you repeatedly experience, what you do not have and how far you can go. The barrier between two seasons is called agreement, but in order to cross this chasm, you first need knowledge, and you come into agreement with that knowledge through the process of understanding. Every consumer is locked in a particular realm of a season. There are five levels of a season; they are:

Class One	Rookie/Beginner
Class Two	Student/Advanced Beginner
Class Three	Tutor/Mentor
Class Four	Teacher
Class Five	Principal

The principal of a season sets the principles of that season, but get this—whenever you master a season, you have to be willing to graduate from that season in order to become a rookie of your next season; this is what it means to humble yourself. It means to go low. Most people are not willing to move on because of fear and pride. You see, being a principal or professor of a season comes with certain benefits. For example, everyone looks up to you; you can, in so many ways, become a celebrity of that particular season, especially within a confined space. All the same, you know your way around that mindset, so you learn to master people by mastering the culture and norms of that mindset or even establishing new norms and customs. When people lock themselves in seasons, those seasons become beautifully decorated prisons, otherwise known as comfort zones. All the same, anytime a person masters a comfort zone, that person, by default, becomes relatively manipulative; this again is because that individual has learned to master the people in that season. This doesn't mean that the individual becomes malicious and/or evil; it simply means that the person recycles the knowledge he or she has acquired. The ones who become the infamous "crabs in a bucket" are the master manipulators or bullies of a season. Think about any confined space where there is the concept of seniority. What have you experienced in some of these spaces? You've likely found yourself being shunned, bullied or sabotaged by one of the principals of that season; this means that the person, in essence, becomes a principality of that season. Master manipulators are oftentimes competitive, and they will punish, sabotage and compete with anyone they deem to be a threat. This is because they can discern between leaders and followers, and they know that anyone who has the potential to lead could potentially master that season and either:

1. Leave them behind.
2. Establish a new set of principles.

And it is for this reason that they will intentionally drive people out of that confined space if they feel that those people will eradicate the systems and subcultures they've built within the spaces or seasons they've mastered. Please note that when God opens the door for us to move on to the next level, and we refuse to go forth, it is almost always because:

1. We are fearful, meaning we lack faith, and according to the scriptures, without faith, we cannot please God.

2. We are not willing to forsake what's familiar to us for our assignments. When you choose what's familiar over your assignment, the familiar becomes the forbidden.

3. We've idolized that season and/or someone in that season.

4. We've fainted (given up) and decided to climax where we are.

5. We're entitled; we don't want the hard work associated with ascending from one realm or region of thought to another, but instead, believe that our seniority with God and our hardships (either present or past tense) entitle us to the next level.

The objective is to keep moving as long as God is ushering you forth and opening doors, but the truth is, we can and do experience trauma during the growth processes in every season. Consequently, we often need wise counsel to push past our fears in order to exit one season and enter into the hallway of the next season. The hallway between two seasons is called the wilderness. It is the space of time that God utilizes to deliver us from the residue of our last seasons and purify us for the next season. But let's talk about the crabs in a bucket!

The crab mentality is one of entitlement; it is birthed from jealousy, fear of rejection and entitlement. Check out the following article about this phenomenal:

> "Crab mentality is a phenomenon where people react negatively, in terms of their thoughts, statements, or actions, to those who get ahead of them, even though they don't expect there to be direct benefits to doing so. For example, crab mentality can cause someone to discourage or sabotage their friend who is starting to do well at school, simply because they're bitter about struggling with their own studies" (Source: Effectiviology/When People Pull Down Those Who Get Ahead).

Again, every consumer is locked in one of the five realms of a season:

Class One	Rookie/Beginner
Class Two	Student/Advanced Beginner
Class Three	Tutor/Mentor
Class Four	Teacher
Class Five	Principal

Whenever you meet people, one of the first things you want to determine before placing an intimate or not-so-intimate label on them is whether or not they are consumers or producers. Most people will fall into the category of a consumer, and again, consumers are not all bad, but they are typically in survival mode, and while they won't necessarily take from one another too much, they will take from people they deem to be better off than themselves. Consumers can be amazing, loyal and faithful friends to other consumers, but remember, they aren't necessarily loyal to people; most people, both consumers and producers alike, are loyal to seasons (mindsets). And the consumers who are more likely to have the crab mentality are the Class Five (Principal) consumers and the Class Four (Teacher) consumers. But, get this—they are oftentimes not the ones who will directly attempt to sabotage your movement; they use what's referred to in the world of psychology as "flying monkeys." What is a flying monkey? Check out the following information:

"Anyone who remembers watching the Wizard of Oz as a child will probably remember how horrifying the Wicked Witch of the West's flying monkeys were. These monkeys were sent by the witch to do her dirty work, and the phrase has since become synonymous with people who end up doing the dirty work of a narcissist.

Flying monkeys get caught up in a narcissist's plan — often to damage the life of another person. The narcissist may use their flying monkeys as piggy in the middle, carrying information from party to party. The flying monkey may use gaslighting tactics, open aggression, and guilt-tripping in order to make another person feel bad and weak, whilst shoring up the narcissist. And they're often involved in pleading the case of the narcissist. Narcissists love having at least one flying monkey, as it makes them feel important and means they can appear to be above the people below them (on both sides) who are caught up in the messy parts of the drama.

The narcissist often recruits his or her flying monkeys from among other family members, such as siblings, spouses, or children. Close friends or work colleagues may also become flying monkeys: I'm sure we've all come across bosses or political leaders who wouldn't be able to function without a band of helpers prepared to get their hands dirty" (Source: Psychology Today/Are You a Narcissist's Flying Monkey?/Claire Jack, Ph.D.).

This is where classes one to three come in. Some of the people from these groups will often look up to the Class Fiver and seek to win favor with that person. And understand this—the Class Fiver does not have to verbally tell his or her followers (flying monkeys) to attack another person; they simply model how they want you to be treated because they know that everyone who admires them or believes that they are the key to their next levels will follow after their lead. For example, if a Class Fiver repeatedly ignores you, stopping to greet everyone else but you, you will notice that the people who follow or look up to the Class Fiver will also ignore you. What's the goal here? Without going too deep into demonology, we must first consider Ephesians 6:12, which reads, "For we wrestle not against flesh and blood, but against principalities, against powers, against the rulers of the darkness of this world, against spiritual wickedness in high places." This means that while we see people acting out, the truth of the matter is that the people who behave this way are in desperate need of deliverance, but their deliverance is found in their obedience to God (see James 4:7). In other words, as long as they refuse to elevate and move into the next chapter of their assignments, they will remain in bondage. Therefore, the attack itself is demonic. Demons use people to hurt, delay and sabotage other people. With that being said, the goal is to cause you to feel rejected. Rejection is the strongman in most deliverances. Rejection can be excruciating, especially when you're new to a season and desperately want to meet and glean from other people. So, the enemy uses them to open you up for the spirit of rejection; this way, you will avoid doing anything that would cause them to feel challenged or intimidated. These are the proverbial crabs in a bucket, but these are the not-so-familiar ones. The most dangerous ones are oftentimes family members, friends or anyone who has intimate access to you.

Now, let's talk about roles. If you happen to be a producer, you have to know that many of the consumers you come in contact with will give you roles and rules that are beneficial to them, meaning they will set the stage for a bunch of one-sided relationships. This is because consumers spend quite a bit of time in "survival mode." In other words, they are driven by demand or need. For example, when I was growing up, my parents were always in survival mode, and everyone they surrounded themselves with was in this state of mind. I had an aunt who was what we called "well-off," which meant that she was either wealthy or relatively prosperous. That particular aunt didn't have a relationship with my parents or with most, if not all, of her siblings. I questioned why she'd stopped talking to us, and I remember that the general explanation I got was that she thought she was better than us. This is a statement that we often hear in poverty-stricken communities regarding people who have distanced themselves from the people they grew up around. And, of course, I started believing this rhetoric as well.

Years later, I found myself going through a divorce and desperately needing money because I was about to lose my house to foreclosure, my car was on the verge of being repossessed and my bills were mounting. So, in addition to my job at AT&T, I decided to sell Mary Kay. I was on the phone with my mother one day when she mentioned this particular aunt of mine. She said that my aunt has always loved Mary Kay and that I should get in contact with her to see if she'd be interested in buying some from me. Pay attention to what I just said! This means that while this aunt was relatively distant from the family, she was definitely accessible. I thought she wanted nothing to do with us. So, I got my aunt's phone number from my mother and I reached out to her. She was excited to hear my voice, and she happily told me to stop by her shop. She said that she needed a new Mary Kay agent. I was excited because when I was a child, I absolutely adored this aunt. We reconnected, and after visiting her shop a few times, she felt comfortable enough to let me in on why she'd distanced herself from the family. Besides her religious beliefs, she'd had a few financial riffs with the family. You see, one of the most frustrating labels a person can wear in the midst of consumers is often framed with these words, "She got money." In this, the individual loses his or her identity to the family and becomes an object of sorts.

First and foremost, let's reestablish this fact—poverty, contrary to popular belief, is not a physical reality; it is a mindset. I know this because I grew up in it, and I was surrounded by this mindset for the majority of my life! The lack of money is simply the fruit of that mindset. In order for a person to escape poverty (the right way), that person has to have a change of heart. This change is rarely welcomed in the communities that they are in because it is hard for us as humans to label what we don't understand. In truth, I've found that there are many labels out there to help us understand the different types of people, personalities and seasons, but every level has a limited amount of labels. For example, I remember standing in front of my mother, my sister and the man I was married to. I felt like they'd all teamed up against me one day, so I'd left the house to go for a walk. When I returned to my mother's house, we somehow started discussing the very reason I had been offended. I remember either my mom or my sister referring to me as "controlling." The man I was married to happily agreed. This was frustrating and confusing because I'd literally never tried to control any of them. I've always been a proponent of choice, but at the same time, I have boundaries. So, I asked them all to give me examples of incidents when I'd tried to control them. I was sincerely ready to conduct a heart check, but the Lord laid it upon my heart to ask them for examples. They didn't have any! They all agreed with the statement my mother made, which was (paraphrased), "When someone tries to tell you to do something, you won't do it." I looked around at everyone, waiting for more examples, but they all latched onto that statement. I then explained what control was to them. I said, "That's not control; those are boundaries." In that moment, the Lord ministered to me, letting me know that they had a limited amount of labels. They simply did not know how to diagnose my personality, so they grabbed the label that made the most sense to them. I learned that day that people see boundaries as an attempt to control them when, in truth, it's an attempt (in many cases) to preserve your relationship with them and stop them from controlling you. So again, everyone has had a certain measure of access to the world and the people in it, and the only labels each person has is dependent upon where that person has been. People who have not gone out much or had a lot of encounters outside their communities often have a limited view of the world because they have a limited amount of labels to identify people with. This often leads to offense. So, saying that a woman, for example, "think she's better" than others is, in most cases, mislabeling the woman simply because the people labeling her cannot relate to or understand her. This is why Amos 3:3 says, "Can two walk together, except they be agreed?"

Going back to the topic at hand—poverty is a mindset. Let's say, for example's sake, that you lived beneath the poverty level. Nevertheless, you decided you didn't want to spend the rest of your life broke. First and foremost, the first sign that you are not only about to break up with a mindset and a reality, but also that you are qualified for a new heart and a new mind is dissatisfaction! Dissatisfaction is oftentimes a green light to success. So, you purchased a few books about financial management, started listening to Dave Ramsey's podcast and you've started hanging around people you can relate to (more on this later). At first, everything feels frustrating because the problem with comfort zones, also known as cycles, is that they stop us from using our problem-solving abilities, and when something is not frequently used, it begins to shrink and weaken (think muscles). In other words, cycles make us weak-minded to the point where we don't like being stretched or challenged. This causes us to become easily offended, frustrated and more likely to quit whenever a certain amount of pressure is placed on us. Nevertheless, you push your way through the discomfort, the many fears and all of the obstacles that come your way. What you will soon discover is that the people you normally hang around will start to notice a change in you, and many of them won't be too favorable of the new you that's emerging. Some people will punish you, but not without first saying, "You've been acting funny!" Again, this is an improper label; it simply means that the person or people in question are losing their abilities to walk with or relate to you simply because your mind is growing. You see, when you're stuck in a realm or a cycle, you tend to recycle old information; this is why people fall into the traps of gossip, unforgiveness and barren conversations. As you continue on your journey to a better you, you will notice that some of the people around you are becoming easily agitated with you. This is because they are starting to feel the sting of rejection. Even though you haven't verbally rejected them, when you chose to grow, you essentially rejected them. And again, some of the people closest to you may respond by "putting you on punishment." What does this punishment look like?

- Not answering your calls.
- Not returning your calls.
- Being relatively dry when speaking to you.
- Ending their conversations with you prematurely.
- Criticizing you, your choices or your new friends.
- Giving you an ultimatum.
- Gossiping about you.
- Lying on you.
- Revealing something you said in confidentiality in an attempt to sabotage your progression.
- Gathering together without you, and then posting it to social media to send you a clear message.
- Attempting or planning to physically assault you.

This is to say that the process of leaving one season can be mentally taxing; this is why we all need therapists to help us to adjust to the many changes and pastors to help us to understand the many changes. We also need mentors that can help to give us language for the many changes that we have experienced and are experiencing; this way, we don't end up delaying our exits from old seasons and our entrances into new seasons.

The aunt who my family considered to be "well-off" welcomed me with open arms. After some time, she began to warn me about some of the people in my family. She said to me, "Tiffany, I can tell that you are going to do great things. Don't you let those folks take advantage of you in the name of family!" I assured her that I wouldn't. This was after she'd shared a few stories of some of my family members attempting to break into her car, vandalize her shop and defame her character simply because she'd said no to them. Remember what I said earlier. The most dangerous label you can have in poverty-stricken communities or amongst people with crab mentalities is the relative "with money" because when people cannot relate to you, they will oftentimes objectify you. Objectification is a dangerous perspective to have in regards to a person or a group of people. It almost always precedes murder! And while that aunt poured knowledge into me during that season, her time in my life would prove to be short-lived. She eventually stopped communicating with me, and I speculated that it was because I'd refused to convert to her religion after she'd attempted a few times to draft me in. Regardless, I appreciated the impartation, and I went on with my life.

Putting the right labels on your relationships will keep you from having the wrong people too close and it will help you to better understand/accept that while some people may serve as blessings in your life, they will be temporary fixtures (seasonal). Their assignment is just to make or receive an impartation and move on. And finally, don't allow the hurt and rejection from others to keep you loyal to a season that God simply wants you to pass through. When you come across Class Fivers, love on them and treat them like the royalty they are, understanding that God may want to use you to help them get free from their insecurities of their fear of the next season.

Objectification

The word "objectification" is defined by Oxford Languages this way, "the action of degrading someone to the status of a mere object." Understand this—God planted a tree in the midst of His garden called the Tree of the Knowledge and Good and Evil. He then commanded Adam and Eve not to eat from this tree. Of course, we know the story. They were tempted by the devil, and they ate fruit from the tree. God then evicted them from the Garden of Eden, and mankind has been trying to find his way back to God ever since. Thankfully, Jesus came along and we are now reconciled to God through His shed blood. Howbeit, the million-dollar question is—why did God put the Tree of the Knowledge of Good and Evil in the midst of the garden? Why didn't He plant this particular tree somewhere else, outside of the couple's reach? The answer is in our makeup.

1. We were created in the image of God.
2. We have a soul, and our souls are comprised of our minds, wills and emotions.
3. There's no point in giving us the ability to make a choice (will) if we don't have anything to choose from.

In short, God wanted us to choose Him on our own. He did not and does not want to control us. Genesis 3:1-7 tells the story. It reads, "Now the serpent was more subtil than any beast of the field which the LORD God had made. And he said unto the woman, Yea, hath God said, Ye shall not eat of every tree of the garden? And the woman said unto the serpent, We may eat of the fruit of the trees of the garden: But of the fruit of the tree which is in the midst of the garden, God hath said, Ye shall not eat of it, neither shall ye touch it, lest ye die. And the serpent said unto the woman, Ye shall not surely die: For God doth know that in the day ye eat thereof, then your eyes shall be opened, and ye shall be as gods, knowing good and evil. And when the woman saw that the tree was good for food, and that it was pleasant to the eyes, and a tree to be desired to make one wise, she took of the fruit thereof, and did eat, and gave also unto her husband with her; and he did eat. And the eyes of them both were opened, and they knew that they were naked; and they sewed fig leaves together, and made themselves aprons."

What we can extract from this story is this:

1. The couple had been given the mechanism of will-power and Satan knew this.

2. Satan, the father of all lies, told the couple 99 percent truths, but he inserted a lie in there as he always does. He said that they wouldn't die if they ate from the tree. This was clearly a lie. Nevertheless, their eyes were opened, and they did become as gods (see Psalms 82:6).

3. In reality, Satan was offering Eve the ability to be independent of God or, better yet, to be her own god.

4. In this, the woman's will was activated and she now had a choice. She could obey God or she could

become independent of Him. She chose the latter; the same is true of her husband.

5. Rejection entered mankind, not because God rejected man, but because man rejected God.

6. Mankind now gets to experience both good and evil, and we can decide which route we want to take. This pretty much answers one of the most asked questions out there, which is—why does God allow evil on Earth? He gave us dominion over the Earth, and He will not usurp that dominion (authority). The Bible tells us that whatever we bind (disallow) on Earth is bound (disallowed) in Heaven, and whatever we loose (allow) on Earth is loosed (allowed) in Heaven (see Matthew 18:18).

Here are a few facts about objectification to consider:

1. It is centered around hatred; it reduces humans down to mere objects.

2. It is the very stuff that serial killers are made of! It silences the moral fabric that covers the human conscious, thus allowing killers to murder others without feeling guilt and shame.

3. Promiscuity is oftentimes the first stage of objectification.

4. Porn watchers objectify people. Please note that it is not possible to see people as sex objects without first objectifying them.

5. Narcissists objectify people, especially those who allow the narcissists to get close to them.

6. Every school shooter that has ever shot up a school was and is guilty of objectification.

7. Divorce is typically centered around objectification. You see, when pride enters the equation, it causes the individual hosting it to lift their desires, wants and needs above that of their spouses, but in order to do this, they have to mislabel their spouses. For example, a man may start labeling his wife as a nag. Of course, this is a bad label, and by doing this, he fails to identify her by her name and her true nature. Once he refers to her as a nag, by instinct, he will begin to mentally disassociate himself from her. Counseling helps to restore marriages by causing the people in them to focus on the fact that their partners are human.

8. Sex traffickers objectify people.

9. People who stand by and record others getting assaulted are guilty of objectification.

10. In summary, objectification is the absence of love eclipsed by an overabundance of selfishness. It means to have Satan's heart for people.

Understand this—Satan sees people as objects. He wants us to serve him, but we are made in the image of God (love), so he wants to remove us from God (since he can't move God away from us); this way, he can manipulate, control and rule over us. God, on the other hand, not only gave us will, He gave us options; this way, we can utilize and strengthen our will. This is similar to some marriages. Let's create two characters: Henry and his wife, Megan. The couple has been married for seven years, but recently, Henry has been relatively cold towards his wife. He's super sensitive, oftentimes annoyed with her, he doesn't seem to want to spend any time with her and he has been coming home a lot later than he usually does. Megan suspects that her husband is having an affair, but she can't prove this, especially given the fact that whenever she did confront Henry, he claimed that he has always been faithful. He also claims that it is his wife's insecurities that make him stay out a little longer than usual. Megan knows better, so she decides to conduct an investigation of her own. Since the cell phones are in her name, Megan reaches out to the cell phone provider and orders detailed billing. She also has the bill sent to her mother's address to ensure that her husband is not privy to her new scheme. All the same, Megan purchases and places a tracker on her husband's vehicle. And the third part of her investigation involves monitoring Henry's social media pages. After a couple of months, Megan has all the evidence she needs to confront her husband, but knowing Henry, she realizes that he'll explain it all away, and then leave her in an attempt to teach her a lesson. In other words, this would be a power move designed to teach her not to check up on him. So, Megan hires a private investigator to confirm every piece of evidence she's uncovered thus far. Two weeks later, Megan gets a call from the investigator, asking her to meet him in the parking lot of a popular grocery store. She agrees. Once she arrives, she gets in the car with the investigator and watches nearly two hours of video and photo evidence of her husband's infidelities. The investigator has captured a video of Henry going to and from a local hotel, he's captured him kissing a woman at a beach, and he has more than an hour of videotape of the couple parking Henry and Megan's car in a wooded area. He also shared photos of Henry purchasing roses for his lover and even visiting her parents' house. This means that Henry is in a full-blown affair, and by full-blown, I mean that he's having both a physical affair and an emotional one. He's also having a financial affair. Megan has all the evidence that she needs. She takes this evidence and confronts her husband with it, but instead of being apologetic, he casts himself as a victim. "Why would you hire someone to follow me around, and why are you monitoring my every move?! This is why I started hanging out with her in the first place! Have fun finding someone who'd be willing to tolerate your crap!" Henry then grabs the keys to his car and walks out the door. As he walks away, he shouts, "I'll be back tomorrow to get my things!" And with those words, he pulls off.

What's happening here? The short answer is—Henry was given the same test and opportunity that Eve had been given in the Garden of Eden. He was given what I call the test of options. You see, there are no perfect people, but whenever you come across narcissistic or toxic people, they highlight the imperfections of others in their attempts to guilt-trip their victims. What's the purpose of guilt-tripping? Why didn't Henry just walk away? To understand this, you must understand the psyche of the human. Whenever a person is guilty of offending or hurting another person, that individual is cognizant of the damage that he or she is doing. In Henry's case, his frustration with his wife is centered around his desire to, as some would say, "have his cake and eat it too." In other words, Henry wanted the privilege of having two women, but because he has already secured his wife, to him, she is of less value; that is unless she repeatedly proves herself to be valuable through works. Howbeit, the other woman is still a forbidden fruit; she is a blank slate or somewhat of a mystery that Henry wants to investigate. She still has buttons he hasn't pushed, beliefs he hasn't explored and insecurities he hasn't discovered. In other words, there are some "benefits" he has yet to enjoy. Nevertheless, he doesn't want to lose his wife, even though he plans to leave her and potentially file for divorce if she doesn't back off and allow him to continue his affair in peace. In truth, Henry doesn't want a divorce; he simply wants time to discover and conquer the other woman, and from there, he wants to go between both women. You see, Henry has managed to silence his conscious, but when this happened, his wife became the voice of reason in his life, and now he wants to silence her. Why am I sharing this? It's simple. To show you an up close and personal look at objectification. Henry didn't start off objectifying his wife, but in order for him to pursue a relationship with his mistress, he had to devalue his wife in his own heart. During the devaluation process, Henry had to attach a series of negative labels to his wife in order to silence the voice of his conscious. Over time, he began to believe all of the negative rhetoric he's told himself. This allowed him to move over into the realm of objectification. And once a person begins to objectify another person, that individual becomes a murderer at heart.

I shared those pointers to help you to better understand just what objectification is. The following information was taken from a paper written by Amelie Pedneault, a student or former student at SFU. It is about renowned serial killer, Ted Bundy:

"The first relevant theme to explore relative to Bundy is his choice of victims, and the way his discourse constructs meaning around their role in his story. Most of his known victims were young females in their twenties, while his very last victim was only 12 years old. One topic that recurred often in his discourse is the metaphor of "women as images". Excerpt 1 – March 27, 1981 "We sent men to Viet Nam and they were able to kill, because the tactics taken by their leaders was to depersonalize the enemy. You're not killing a man; you're killing a "gook," a Viet Cong. Under those circumstances, men kill very easily. Certainly the situation we're discussing does not have the legitimacy or atmosphere of war. And yet, the same psychological mechanisms are used by a person who kills indiscriminately – except he is not killing a person. He is killing an image." (Michaud & Aynesworth, 1989, p. 69)

This excerpt constitutes a clear illustration of dehumanization of the victim. His victims are no longer living and breathing human beings they are images. This objectification of his victims presents the use of a first neutralization technique – the denial of the victim. Also, his use of an analogy comparing the situation of a serial killer to that of soldier going at war for his country is explicit. By the description of a situation that the reader can

relate with (i.e., war), he invites the reader to a deepened understanding of his own situation (Source: Simon Fraser University/Ted Bundy on the "Malignant Being":
An Analysis of the Justificatory Discourse of a Serial Killer/Amelie Pednault).

What's the point of this lesson? We are seeing the rapid growth of narcissism in this era, and according to the Bible, things won't get any better. Matthew 24:9-14 reads (in reference to the last days), Then shall they deliver you up to be afflicted, and shall kill you: and ye shall be hated of all nations for my name's sake. And then shall many be offended, and shall betray one another, and shall hate one another. And many false prophets shall rise, and shall deceive many. And because iniquity shall abound, the love of many shall wax cold. But he that shall endure unto the end, the same shall be saved. And this gospel of the kingdom shall be preached in all the world for a witness unto all nations; and then shall the end come." Notice that the scripture says "the love of many shall wax cold." This means that we will see a decline in love and an incline in objectification. Isn't this what we're witnessing right now? Capitalism is a form of objectification! I share this so that you can understand the importance of following 1 John 4:1, which reads, "Beloved, believe not every spirit, but try the spirits whether they are of God: because many false prophets are gone out into the world." Believe it or not, a lot of the people who will approach you in this event that we call life will not have a heart of love. They will be opportunists, people who see what you can add to their lives, not considering what they will take away from yours. This is where relational acuity comes in. You have to have the ability to examine the fruits of the people who audition for a role in your life. All the same, it is not wise for you to try and audition for a part in someone's life without first utilizing the power of prayer and examination. For example, I like to study people from afar and I've learned not to rush into any relationships, be they platonic or romantic. I've learned the power and benefits of setting boundaries. Having relational intelligence means being patient, but first, you must establish good fruits in your own life.

Most of the traumas we've experienced in life are the results of us not testing the spirits of the people we've entertained. You see, one of the most common (and ignored) red flags is when a person rushes a relationship. For example:

1. That girl who calls you her friend or best friend within days or weeks of you meeting her.
2. That guy who proclaims his love for you within days or weeks of dating him.
3. That pastor who left the pulpit just to give you a prophetic word the first day you stepped foot into his or her church (Note: this isn't always a bad thing, but understand narcissistic leaders do this in an attempt to obligate you to their churches. Good and Godly leaders won't try to prophesy themselves into your life.)
4. That family member who you haven't spoken with in years who suddenly wants to reconnect. He or she

tries to rush back into the seat of familiarity in your life, not realizing that you have to get to know him or her all over again.

5. That ex who inboxes you, using flattery and trying to pry his or her way back into your life. (The fact that this person is an ex should be a big enough red flag).

My point is—don't allow people to enter into your life and into your intimate space who have no ability to love or appreciate the gem that you are. Don't allow yourself to become an object. To prevent this from happening, you have to employ relational acuity. This includes:

1. **Testing the spirit:** This is done through prayer, time and distance. And by distance, I mean that you shouldn't bring people close until you've had enough time to examine their fruits and learn the patterns in their lives.

2. **Guarding your heart:** This is done by you not relinquishing intimate information prematurely. All the same, don't allow people to love-bomb you or rush you into a relationship with them. And don't feel guilty about having boundaries! Emotionally healthy people won't be offended at the sight of your boundaries because they are patient and understand why boundaries are needed. Nevertheless, bound people hate boundaries; they will get offended and cast themselves as (1) victims and (2) blessings in an attempt to get you to lower your standards.

3. **Loving God and yourself:** Luke 10:25-27 tells a

familiar story. It reads, "And, behold, a certain lawyer stood up, and tempted him, saying, Master, what shall I do to inherit eternal life? He said unto him, What is written in the law? How readest thou? And he answering said, Thou shalt love the Lord thy God with all thy heart, and with all thy soul, and with all thy strength, and with all thy mind; and thy neighbour as thyself." One of the most valuable lessons and powerful weapons you'll ever have the pleasure of yielding is love. But love is made perfect in Christ only. This is why Matthew 6:33 says, "But seek ye first the kingdom of God, and his righteousness; and all these things shall be added unto you." When we learn to love God with everything that we are and all that we have, we then, by default and instinct, learn to love ourselves. This love is what waters the fruits of the Spirit. It also helps us to be more inept at testing spirits, setting boundaries and walking away from any and everything that does not reflect God's love.

Lastly, relational acuity is NOT:
- Feeling sorry for someone and allowing that person to take advantage of you repeatedly simply because you pity the individual.
- Allowing toxic people to remain in your life because you're afraid to be alone or start over.
- Tolerating evil or broken people because you are benefiting in some way from your relationship with them.
- Loving others more than you love yourself. The

Bible tells us to love others "as" or in the same manner in which we love ourselves.

GENERALIZATION

The word "generalization" comes from the word "generalize," and according to Cambridge Dictionary, it is defined as "to make a general statement that something is true in all cases, based on what is true in some cases." Examples of generalization include, but are not limited to:

1. Assuming that everyone or the majority of people from a specific race behaves a certain way or is prone to certain behaviors.
2. Assuming and promoting the idea that all men or women are the same.
3. Assuming that all cops are bad.
4. Assuming that all mother-in-laws are evil.
5. Assuming that all stepparents are villains.

Of course, these are just a few examples of generalization. Please note that generalization can be a life-saving tool in some instances. For example, an older woman assumes that every man who "pimps" when he walks may be a potential threat to her. So, while walking out of a shopping center one day, she locks eyes with a man whose appearance makes her uncomfortable. As he walks, she notices that he's willfully limping (pimp-walking). She then avoids him by getting off the sidewalk and heading towards her car. While he may be a good and decent guy, this is her version of discernment, and believe it or not, it may potentially save her life someday. Of course, this may be a form of racism if the woman is of a different race than the guy in question; then again, if she belongs to the same race, we may consider her choice to avoid the guy a form of ignorance. Howbeit, if we put pressure on every woman to ignore what she believes to be discernment, we will essentially put them in danger. If we educate them, however, we can deal a devastating blow to generalization as a whole. Also note that the word "ignorant" comes from the root word "ignore." It simply means that information is present, but we choose to ignore it. Ignorance, of course, is a willful act.

The following information was taken from Fandom.com:
> "Learned generalization or secondary generalization is an aspect of learning theory. In learning studies it can be shown that subjects, both animal and human will respond in the same way to different stimuli if they have similar properties established by a process of conditioning. This underpins the process by which subjects are able to perform newly acquired behaviors in new settings. This was formalized in Roger Shepard's universal law of generalization which states the probability that a response to one stimulus will be generalized to another will be a function of the distance between the two stimuli. "Generalization" in this case is measured by means of confusion error, while the use of "distance" depends on the assumption that stimuli will be compared in some kind of psychological space (the latter being typical of Shepard's work).

Using experimental evidence from both human and non-human subjects, Shepard hypothesizes, more specifically, that probability of generalization will fall off exponentially with the distance measured by one of two particular metrics. His analysis goes on to argue for the universality of this rule for all sentient organisms due to evolutionary internalization" (Source: Fandom.com/Generalization (learning).

To make this easier to understand, let's look at another definition; this time, from the Psychology Dictionary. "Deriving a concept or theory from a number of specific cases, applying it widely. 2. Judgment derived and applied this way. 3. Conditioning process where a response is evoked by the same stimuli" (Source: Psychology Dictionary/Generalization).

Why is the topic of generalization important in the area of relational intelligence? Because the goal here is so that we can all grow in our intelligence as it relates to relationships. And people who typically generalize other people are oftentimes broken, hurting and toxic. Remember the popular adage, "Hurt people hurt people." For example, let's say that you are a single woman who meets and exchanges numbers with a single man. At first, all appears to be well. He calls you often, wants to spend time with you and his interest in you is evident. At some point during your relationship to and with him, he starts calling you "baby" instead of referring to you by your name. This isn't alarming, given the fact this behavior is relatively common and maybe even expected nowadays. However, one day, you offend him by telling him that you'll be going on a cruise with a few friends. Now, keep in mind that the two of you are not married. You are simply two people who are in the dating phase of your relationship with one another. As it turns out, your new beau has trust issues. He thinks that an all-girls' cruise means that you and your friends will be getting drunk, partying and exchanging numbers with random guys. He even thinks that you may be willing to engage in a one-night stand with some handsome guy in another country. He reasons that this is why you didn't bother to invite him on the cruise. So, the two of you argue, and in the middle of that argument, you notice that he's no longer calling you "baby." As a matter of fact, he's not even referring to you by your first name. Instead, he proclaims, "Y'all women are always talking about you want a good man, but when you get one, this is how you act!" This is the language of generalization, and it signifies that he has some unresolved traumas as it relates to women, especially in the arena of romance. One of the most common and dangerous beliefs that many women have is that they can prove to a man like this that not all women are cheaters. They plan to do this by:

1. Repeatedly comforting their guys whenever they have jealous episodes.
2. Reassuring their guys whenever their insecurities flare up.
3. Giving their guys access to everything that they have, including passwords for their phones, social media accounts, etc.
4. Telling their guys about every conversation they

have, especially the conversations about the guys in question.

5. Sabotaging or ending any and every relationship that makes their guys uncomfortable.

Remember these words—you can't talk a demon out of being a demon! Also, you can't fit into the God-sized hole in another person's heart, after all, the war is not against flesh and blood. The scriptures tell us that it is against powers, principalities and the rulers of this dark world, including spiritual wickedness in high places (see Ephesians 6:12). Consider 2 Corinthians 10:5, which reads, "Casting down imaginations, and every high thing that exalteth itself against the knowledge of God, and bringing into captivity every thought to the obedience of Christ." Also, consider Proverbs 25:28, which reads, "He that hath no rule over his own spirit is like a city that is broken down, and without walls." A city broken down and without walls has no protection from the enemy. The city here is our hearts; this is what God told us to guard. An unguarded heart is the devil's playground. This means that a person who does not guard his or her heart is a person who will likely hear many voices; these includes the voices of demons and the voices of the people they surround themselves with. This is what makes them double-minded and unstable. This is why I warn people with these words—never give people access to your heart when they don't know how to guard their own. Imagine telling a guy that you love him, you will always be faithful to him, you will never leave him and that you are satisfied with him (if you're a man, imagine saying this to a woman). Now, imagine that the man or woman in question doesn't know how to guard his or her heart. So, the individual receives your words with gladness, but as soon as the guy (or girl) is away from you, another voice comes and says, "She's only saying this because you are onto her games. She's like every other woman. I bet she's on the phone making plans with her secret lover right now!" Now, the guy (or girl) in question is right back angry with you.

Always listen for the sounds or evidence of generalization. This isn't to say that you should cast away everyone who displays ignorance in an area; it is to say that if you notice that this is a pattern for the individual or if you fit into the category that the individual generalizes, you should be mindful that you don't bring that person too close to your heart. A good example is a woman who believes that:
1. Every married man is a cheater.
2. Every man wants her.

Believe it or not, this is a form of trauma. Her trauma response may be arrogance. Please understand that over-the-top, flamboyant and flagrant attitudes are nothing but the swelling of one's ego. This swelling was induced by trauma. You see, whenever we are traumatized, we stop growing in the areas that we were impacted in; that is if we do not get the help we need to heal properly. In this particular woman's case, she was likely genuinely hurt by a woman or a group of women who were jealous of her. Understand that jealousy is rooted in fear; typically, it's the fear of rejection, the fear of abandonment or the fear of being overlooked. Does this mean that every woman who dislikes her or distances themselves from her is jealous? Absolutely not! Get this—there is what I call the "vampiric effect." It simply means that you will become the very thing that hurt you if you don't heal properly. Think about vampire movies. The goal of a vampire bite was to turn those who were bitten into vampires or to kill them altogether. In this, the woman in question also becomes relatively fearful, but her fear may not manifest like those of her villains. Instead, she begins to see the world through a warped lens. She begins to reason that she is a victim of her own beauty. This causes her to quietly fear relationships with other women. If deeply rooted enough, this fear will eventually cause her to objectify other women. So again, let's say that this particular woman, albeit beautiful, has extremely low self-esteem, even though she is extremely conceited. (Note: conceit and self-esteem are not one and the same. Conceit is typically built on vanity, whereas, self-esteem is typically built on character). Because she believes that every man is a cheater, every man wants her and every woman is jealous of her, she may respond to her trauma by:

1. Having affairs with married men.
2. Posting photos of herself in an attempt to garner the attention of men, and then "exposing" or threatening to expose every married man who dares to inbox her.
3. Make a lot of condescending posts and statements about women. For example, she may say, "I don't know why Black women are so insecure! Listen, I don't want your man! Your man wants me! Ask him!"

4. Isolating herself.
5. Surrounding herself with women who are also beautiful but traumatized. These ladies will typically form a trauma bond around their beliefs; this is how "mean girl" squads are formed.

This is because generalization is the highest expression of trauma. How relational generalization works is:

1. We are traumatized in a particular area.
2. We focus on certain aspects of the person who traumatized us.
3. We are traumatized again in that area.
4. We notice that the person who traumatized us this time bears certain similarities to the person who traumatized us the last time.
5. We notice a pattern of trauma in our lives, and we begin to attribute that trauma to a certain group of people, rather than acknowledging the fact that we have what is referred to as "a type." A type, spiritually speaking, is nothing but a familiar spirit that we have yet to end our relationships with.
6. We stop forming relationships with people who fall into that category, or we form relationships with them, all the while keeping our guards up or trying to control the direction of the relationship by controlling them.

Non-relational generalization includes racism, sexism and pretty much anything that ends with "ism."

MASTERMINDING KINGDOM RELATIONSHIPS

First and foremost, what are Kingdom relationships? In summary, they are bonds developed between believers that help each party to effectively complete his or her assignment on Earth. Make no mistake about it; you have a God-given assignment; you are not just here to take up space and time. Another way to say this is—we all have a purpose, and get this—not all of our purposes or assignments are carried out in church environments. Joseph's assignment was carried out in the castle of a pagan king; the same was true for Queen Esther and Prophet Daniel. Joseph was called to the mountains of government and business, Esther was called to the mountain of government and Daniel was called to the mountains of government and religion. Please note that there are seven societal mountains of influence; they are the mountains of:

1. Arts and Entertainment
2. Media
3. Family
4. Religion
5. Government
6. Education
7. Business

Where did the concept of the seven societal mountains originate? Check out the article below. In Loren

Cunningham's book, Making Jesus Lord , she wrote:

"Sometimes God does something dramatic to get our attention. That's what happened to me in 1975. My family and I were enjoying the peace and quiet of a borrowed cabin in the Colorado Rockies. I was stretched out on a lounge chair in the midday warmth, praying and thinking. I was considering how we Christians – not just the mission I was part of, but all of us – could turn the world around for Jesus. A list came to my mind: categories of society which I believed we should focus on in order to turn nations around to God. I wrote them down, and stuck the paper in my pocket.

The next day, I met with a dear brother, the leader of Campus Crusade For Christ, Dr. Bill Bright. He shared with me something God had given him – several areas to concentrate on to turn the nations back to God! They were the same areas, with different wording here and there, that were written on the page in my pocket. I took it out and showed Bill and we shook our heads in amazement.

Here's a list (refined and clarified a bit over the years) that God gave me that sunny day in Colorado:

1. The home
2. The church
3. Schools
4. Government and politics
5. The media
6. Arts, entertainment, and sports
7. Commerce, science, and technology."

I read a few articles about the Seven Mountain Mandate,

and many of them say that this movement has no biblical basing, but it actually does! Apostle John wrote the following scriptures (through the inspiration of the Holy Spirit, of course):

- **Revelation 12:3:** And there appeared another wonder in heaven; and behold a great red dragon, having seven heads and ten horns, and seven crowns upon his heads.
- **Revelation 13:1:** And I stood upon the sand of the sea, and saw a beast rise up out of the sea, having seven heads and ten horns, and upon his horns ten crowns, and upon his heads the name of blasphemy.
- **Revelation 17:8-9:** The beast that thou sawest was, and is not; and shall ascend out of the bottomless pit, and go into perdition: and they that dwell on the earth shall wonder, whose names were not written in the book of life from the foundation of the world, when they behold the beast that was, and is not, and yet is. And here is the mind which hath wisdom. The seven heads are seven mountains, on which the woman sitteth.

The head represents authority. The seven heads of the beast (Satan) all represent the authority he has over the seven societal mountains of influence. The seven heads represent seven principalities or ruling spirits. The ten crowns represent their rulership over each of these mountains. One of the most powerful lessons I learned about relationships is that no one is truly a friend until that person:

1. Knows, honors and submits to the Most High God.

2. Knows, honors and accepts who he or she is in the Lord.
3. Knows and surrenders to his or her assignment in Christ.

This means that the individual has some measure of clarity as it relates to his or her assignment. In other words, while we don't always have language for the worlds or mountains we're called to, we should all have a rough idea of who we are. This is why the Bible tells us to love our neighbors as we love ourselves. Your neighbors aren't just the people who live next door to you. Your neighbor is everyone who frequents a space in or around your life. The person sitting next to you at church is your neighbor. The individual standing behind you in the checkout line is your neighbor at that moment. The angry driving honking his horn at you is your neighbor. Your spouse is your neighbor. Your children are your neighbors. Everyone you can touch with your arms, see with your eyes, inspire with your creativity, impact with your choices or reach with your voice is a neighbor of yours. This means that you have a direct impact on that person's life, whether that impact is minuscule or highly transformational. Am I saying that the people around you who don't necessarily know and understand their identities and assignments are not truly your friends? Absolutely, but it would depend on your definition of the word "friend." This is because you can only truly love a person to the degree in which you love and understand yourself. All the same, while we pledge our loyalty to people through the use of labels, the truth is that we are truly only loyal to a set of principles. This means that we learn to love people who frequent the same regions of thought that we live in. Therefore, our loyalty is almost always to the principles and not the people. Howbeit, when we truly align ourselves with the voice, will and heart of God, we can truly say that we are friends (by heavenly definition) because it is then and only then that we come fully into agreement with one another. In every other instance, we are simply in agreement in certain areas of our lives about certain things, and as we grow in those areas, we will find ourselves growing closer or growing apart. We grow closer when our principles begin to parallel; we grow apart when our principles are misaligned. But what if I told you that the only way you'll grow in wisdom, remain humble and become multifaceted is if you build relationships with people that you don't always fully agree with? I'm not saying that you need to go out and befriend twisted, perverted and ungodly people. I'm saying that you need to stop limiting yourself to people that you feel comfortable around. Remember, comfort is an enemy of destiny! Consider Joseph's plight. The men who should have protected, understood and loved him hated him. These men were his own brothers! When Joseph found himself in Potiphar's house, Joseph had favor. He had so much favor that Potiphar's wife began to find him irresistible. After this, he found himself in prison, and guess what? His favor followed him there! Please don't think for one second that Potiphar's wife got away with her crime against Joseph. The Bible doesn't tell us what became of Potiphar and his wife, but we do know this— favor follows the favored! This means that the favor of God followed Joseph right out of that house. The residue

of it likely lingered for a few months before dissipating. All
the same, can you imagine how Potiphar and his wife felt
the moment they saw that Joseph was about to reign next
to the king?! This means that he became Potiphar's boss!
And, of course, Joseph found favor with Pharaoh. Am I
saying that you should go out and get yourself some
unsaved friends? No, that's not what I'm saying, after all,
the scriptures tell us:

- **2 Corinthians 6:14:** Be ye not unequally yoked
  together with unbelievers: for what fellowship hath
  righteousness with unrighteousness? And what
  communion hath light with darkness?
- **1 Corinthians 15:33:** Be not deceived: evil
  communications corrupt good manners.
- **James 4:4:** Ye adulterers and adulteresses, know ye
  not that the friendship of the world is enmity with
  God? Whosoever therefore will be a friend of the
  world is the enemy of God.

But wait! Did you know that many believers and religious
organizations have misread the aforementioned
scriptures? In 2 Corinthians 6:14, God tells us to not be
"unequally yoked" with unbelievers. How then can we
minister to them if we can't talk with them? This scripture
is NOT telling us to ignore unsaved people. It literally says
not to be unequally yoked with them. This means that light
is higher than darkness; you are to lead in those
relationships. You shouldn't be intimate with them
because, in friendship, there is an equal pour. Instead,
your relationship with an unbeliever should center around
evangelism. Consider the yoke placed on an animal. Check

out the following article for more insight.

"Animal yokes allow animals to pull farming equipment, like a plow, along with wagons and carriages. The animals most commonly used to pull farm equipment, wagons, and carriages are horses, donkeys, mules, and oxen. The reasons these types of animals are used are due to their strength. Each of these types of animals all has their own merits and faults. Some of the benefits of theses animals are that they can help with a variety of crops, by lowering costs on gas and repairs for tractors, and by creating manure that works as fertilizer. Donkeys are members of the horse family that have adapted to desert areas. The donkey's ancestors are from Africa and the first domestic donkeys can be traced back to around 4000 B.C. and 3000 B.C. in Lower Egypt. Donkeys are considered by many to be a stubborn animal due to their stronger sense of self-preservation. Donkeys unlike the horse, who would be willing to work itself to death, will stop when it feels that it is in danger. Also, unlike the horse and the ox, donkeys tend to be used only for pulling carts, or to carry things on their backs and are prized for their ability to handle steep and rocky terrain. Mules are a produced from the breeding of male donkeys and female horses, but the breeding of a female donkey with a male horse produces a hinny. Mules tend to be larger than donkeys are better able to pull heavy loads.
Oxen are bulls that have been castrated and are usually easier to handle than intact bulls. Oxen are

used in pairs to pull carts and farm equipment. When using animals to pull farm equipment, Oxen tend to be the better of the choices. This is due to their ability to pull heavier things and to work longer than the horse or the donkey, but it will take longer for them to work, because they are slower. Oxen can also help with more than just pulling equipment they can also help with threshing by walking over the grain and they can help power machines for grinding grain. However, they don't make good choices for riding, areas where the horse, mule and donkey excel" (Source: USA Institute of Texan Cultures/A Smithsonian Affiliate/Ox Yoke/Illa Bennett).

Can you imagine yoking a donkey with an ox? Donkeys are stubborn creatures, while oxen are hard workers. To be unequally yoked with an unbeliever means to come under the headship or authority of that person. Consider Joseph's relationship with Pharaoh and Daniel's relationship with Nebuchadnezzar. Both men served as advisors to the king, and not the other way around. The same is true for Esther. While she was the wife of a pagan king, her submission to him caused him to submit to her wise counsel. This doesn't mean we are free to marry unbelievers because the Bible explicitly speaks against this. It does mean that we should not rely on the world's system or the people who are submitted to that system; this is because God called us to be the head or, better yet, the authority. Deuteronomy 28:13 says it this way, "And the LORD shall make thee the head, and not the tail; and thou shalt be above only, and thou shalt not be beneath; if that thou hearken unto the commandments of the LORD thy God, which I command thee this day, to observe and to do them." But wait! We work for the world, right? Most of us have unsaved bosses, or we have to be educated under unsaved teachers and professors. Wouldn't this mean that we should quit our jobs and demand that our teachers be Christian? Absolutely not! It means that we should lead them in Christ, even if we do this through our behavior. The problem occurs when Christians look up to, admire or inspire to be like unbelievers. This puts the unbeliever in the headship or mentorship position. This is what the Bible refers to as the proverbial "blind leading the blind." Proverbs 24:1 warns us this way, "Be not thou envious against evil men, neither desire to be with them." Proverbs 23:1-3 says it best; it reads, "When thou sittest to eat with a ruler, consider diligently what is before thee: and put a knife to thy throat, if thou be a man given to appetite. Be not desirous of his dainties: for they are deceitful meat." What's significant about this particular situation? The person in question is a ruler. The Bible tells us not to desire his dainties; in other words, don't look up to him, otherwise, you'll glean from him and not the other way around. If I come in contact with an unbeliever, I don't have to say to that person, "I can't be your friend because you don't believe in or accept Jesus." Instead, I have to become the embodiment of Christ, meaning I must display the love and character of Christ. All the same, I shouldn't be on the phone, for example, telling the unbeliever my personal problems, nor should I allow the person to engage in evil communication with me. An example of evil communication is when someone details their sins in an agreeable way. I immediately think about an old friend of mine who went back into fornication. She wanted to talk to me about her indiscretions, but I wouldn't allow her to do so. She decided that she was going to force me to listen to her. She'd started trying to talk about her most recent encounter with a guy, so I said, "I don't want to talk about that." After this, she began to yell at me about being "so heavenly minded that I was no earthly good." After she'd fussed for about a minute, she continued, "So yeah, back to the story. He then touched me..." I stopped her again. I said, "Like I said before, I don't want to hear about it. I'm not about to have this conversation with you." I don't remember what happened after that because I almost always seemed to butt heads with this particular friend; that was until I realized that we were unequally yoked. Was she a believer? I thought so at the time, but after we'd parted ways, she walked away from the faith altogether and began to practice witchcraft. David said in Psalm 119:11, "Thy word have I hid in mine heart, that I might not sin against thee." The heart is the centerpiece of the soul. What I've come to understand is this—some people are only saved in language, but they truly have never allowed God in their hearts. This is why Jesus said in Matthew 15:8, "This people draweth nigh unto me with their mouth, and honoureth me with their lips; but their heart is far from me." In truth, I suspect that there will be a lot of people who identify themselves as Christians who will be in for a rude awakening on Judgment Day. In Matthew 7:21-23, Jesus said, "Not everyone who says to Me, 'Lord, Lord,' shall enter the kingdom of heaven, but he who does the will of My Father in heaven. Many will say to Me in that day, 'Lord, Lord, have we not prophesied in Your name, cast out demons in Your name, and done many wonders in Your name?' And then I will declare to them, 'I never knew you; depart from Me, you who practice lawlessness!'" The point is—put everyone in the right positions in your life and never allow yourself to lust after all this world has to offer. There's nothing wrong with wanting nice things, but if you put God first, He will purify your perspective. In other words, you won't desire the treasures and riches of this world to make yourself powerful or to gain the approval/acceptance of others. Instead, everything that you do and acquire will be used to further His Kingdom in the Earth. This also means that if you were to ever find yourself, for example, speaking with one of the world's celebrities or dining with a rich and powerful person, that individual wouldn't have any power over you. You won't lust after what the person has; instead, you will hold true to your faith. Consequently, the individual in question may get saved (if the person isn't already saved). Remember, you shouldn't be under the influence of the world; instead, your assignment is to bring the world under the influence of Jesus. "And I, if I be lifted up from the earth, will draw all men unto me" (John 12:32).

Masterminding Kingdom relationships is all about positioning. Think about a system. When everything is in its proper place, the system can function the way it was designed to function. When one thing is off, on the other hand, the system stalls. Your life is a system. I'll say it this way—you are a word of God, just as Jesus is the Word of God. Everyone you come in contact with is a (lowercase) word of God. And every time you form a connection with a person, the two of you are making a statement. The more relationships you form, the more statements you make, but the key isn't in the quantity of relationships, it's the quality of relationships. You should form bonds or connections with people who heighten God's voice in you, and stay away from people who muzzle your faith, all the while handing a mic to your carnality. Two people who love and pursue the Lord can make a far greater and more significant statement than one thousand people who are not avid students of God's Word. This is why I've never been drawn to crowds. All too often, cliques and crowds don't make sense because many of them are yoked together by perversion and fear. I dare to say this— some of them are nothing but Christian covens that house men and women who love their sins more than they love the Lord, and the glue that holds them together is their disdain for holiness and Godly people. If you truly surrender your heart and will to the Lord, these people will reject you. This is when you will have to come to one of the many crossroads in life; this is when you have to make a significant decision: do you want to continue in your pursuit of God, all the while being rejected by many of your brethren or do you want to fit in? Sadly enough, most people choose the latter. Howbeit, the believers who choose God over people usually have a great degree of humility, and their greatest marker is love, after all, God is Love. These are the people you want to form relationships with, and remember, not all relationships have to be intimate. Some of them can be intellectual. Some of the most valuable connections you'll ever form will fall under the category of intellectual relationships! These are people who are not in your intimate circle, but they add value to your life in one way or another and vice versa. And while you may not be close to them, they are close to God, just as you are. Because of your proximity to God's heart, you won't feel the need to forge an intimate connection with them because, as the old folks used to say, "What's understood does not need to be spoken." They'll know and love you from afar, just as you'll do the same with and for them. And many of these types of relationships alternate between intimate to intellectual. You'll find that in some seasons, you are close to these people, while in other seasons, you may not speak to or hear from them as much. But if you're both mature, neither of you will take offense to this. Instead, you'll learn to do life together in a healthy way, rather than trying to force a connection that doesn't need to be forced. Another way to look at this is—in order for a relationship to be healthy and good, you have to take the religion out of it. This means you have to throw away the rules and requirements that the world taught you to burden one another with. I think about a dear friend of mine who I have not spoken with in about two years, and one thing is for sure, she is my friend! If I call her needing a place to stay, she will readily open her home to me. Are we intimately connected? No. She's more of an intellectual friend (Circle 3), but we've been intimately connected in times' past, meaning we were relatively open with one another about our lives, fears and plans. But even then, she's never been a part of Circle 1, nor have I have held that space in her heart, and guess what? We're both okay with that! While she's in my intellectual circle, I still revere her as a friend.

Below, you'll find ten ways to mastermind Kingdom relationships:

1. Pray about everything and everyone. After this, wait for God to answer before you start putting labels on people.
2. You will know them by their fruits. Study the fruits of the Spirit and the works of the flesh; master them in your own life, and examine them in the lives of others. If your fruit of kindness, for example, is greater than theirs, you are not their friend in that area, you are a mentor!
3. Never form a relationship based on your need, and never allow someone with a need to toss you into their intimate circle simply because they need that need met.
4. Love God with all of your heart, mind and strength, and then learn to love yourself. This way, you can love your neighbors in the same manner in which you love yourself.
5. Identify where everyone is in your life.
6. When you're hurting, don't open up to people in your intellectual circle unless the Lord tells you to do so. Reach out to your wise counselors. If you can't reach them, talk to a mature, God-fearing person in your intimate circle.

7. Don't try to equalize your relationships, and beware of people who don't know how to have hierarchical relationships. Keep them in your intellectual circle, and if they cannot respect that space, don't give them access to your life or heart.

8. Don't get offended when people shift from one circle to the next or out of your life altogether. Movement is a sign of growth!

9. Stop referring to your enemies as friends, and stop treating your friends like your enemies.

10. Always choose your assignment over your relationships, and your relationships will flourish. But, if you choose your relationships over your assignment, you have rejected God in favor of people. This is why there are so many demonized people in the church today. It's not residue from the world. The problem is, they keep choosing people and the things of this world over God. "Because that, when they knew God, they glorified him not as God, neither were thankful; but became vain in their imaginations, and their foolish heart was darkened. Professing themselves to be wise, they became fools, and changed the glory of the uncorruptible God into an image made like to corruptible man, and to birds, and four-footed beasts, and creeping things. Wherefore God also gave them up to uncleanness through the lusts of their own hearts, to dishonour their own bodies between themselves: Who changed the truth of God into a lie, and worshipped and served the creature more than the Creator, who is blessed for ever.

Amen. For this cause God gave them up unto vile affections: for even their women did change the natural use into that which is against nature: And likewise also the men, leaving the natural use of the woman, burned in their lust one toward another; men with men working that which is unseemly, and receiving in themselves that recompence of their error which was meet. And even as they did not like to retain God in their knowledge, God gave them over to a reprobate mind, to do those things which are not convenient; being filled with all unrighteousness, fornication, wickedness, covetousness, maliciousness; full of envy, murder, debate, deceit, malignity; whisperers, backbiters, haters of God, despiteful, proud, boasters, inventors of evil things, disobedient to parents, without understanding, covenantbreakers, without natural affection, implacable, unmerciful: Who knowing the judgment of God, that they which commit such things are worthy of death, not only do the same, but have pleasure in them that do them" (Romans 1:21-32).

God first. You second. Them third. Remember that order. Keep that order. And never be afraid to lose your relationship with a person. Amazingly enough, the greatest form of relational witchcraft is people who get close and then threaten you with their absence. Let them go! The only alternative they are giving you is this—either you let them control you and lead you outside the will of God, muzzling you along the way, OR you can retain your God-given authority and go on in life without them. When people threaten you with their absence, they are demonized, and by resisting their attempts to control you, you are instigating the effects of James 4:7, which reads, "Submit yourselves therefore to God. Resist the devil, and he will flee from you." Not only will the devil flee from you, but the folks who got the devil in them will take flight as well. Over the course of time, you'll come to understand why it was necessary to let them go. As you grow in Christ (if you continue to move from one region of thought to another), you will someday look back and you'll be surprised at how much space and distance (in thought) you are from them. It's surreal to see a person you once looked up to in a low place, but get this—they were always there! Once God increased your height in the realm of the spirit, you were able to see them from a different angle or perspective. This will only inspire you to grow all the more. And people who learn to appreciate growth rarely, if ever, climax in life. This is what keeps their minds sharp, even in their old age. They learned to mastermind their relationships, rather than being mastered by the people they find themselves in relationships with. Do the same and you will come to understand the mysteries of the Kingdom!

Note: Move on to book number two if you want to go deeper!

www.ingramcontent.com/pod-product-compliance
Lightning Source LLC
Chambersburg PA
CBHW072343090426
42741CB00012B/2898